Marketing Smart

A collection of proven marketing strategies
and tips to help Challenger Brands take on
their larger competitors… and win!

written by
John Gumas

Published by:
Gumas Advertising
99 Shotwell Street
San Francisco, CA 94103
Tel: 415-621-7575
Email: jgumas@gumas.com
www.gumas.com

Editor: Jeff Pena

© 2010 John Gumas

ISBN 978-0-557-42700-0

Printed in the U.S.A.

A special thanks to my beautiful wife Janice for putting up with me all these years and for always having a big smile on her face when I come home at night!

And to my kids Nicholas, Alexander and Stephanie…
If a knucklehead like Dad can do this, just
imagine what you guys can do!

Accolades. . .

"Universities highly value wisdom and sage advice, and our alumnus, John Gumas, has shared generously with us over the years. Readers of *Marketing Smart* can now benefit from decades of marketing savvy and community service that have distinguished Gumas' career."
- Robert Corrigan, President, San Francisco State University

"If you're Google, Disney or Coke... don't bother with this book. For the rest of us, it's a must-read – filled with pragmatic, results-delivering insights that will prepare our brands to take on and conquer any competitor."
- Drew McLellan, President, McLellan Marketing Group, Des Moines, IA

"A keen understanding of not just business but how to grow businesses is what John brings to the table. Regardless of your industry or position in your market, John's refreshing and methodical approach to building your market share is a must-read for any executive."
- Del Esparza, President, Esparza Advertising, Albuquerque, NM

"To build a successful Challenger Brand you need to get into a challenger mindset. To market a Challenger Brand you need to outthink, rather than outspend, the competition. John's book, *Marketing Smart,* is what any smart David needs to out-market Goliath."
- Andrew G. Gordon, President, Direct Impact Group, Newton, MA

"John Gumas is a world-class strategic marketer – one of the leading innovators in the business. Gumas consistently delivers breakthrough results for his clients by keeping the work collaborative, fun, leading edge and true to the strategy."
- Leslie Milloy, VP, Dir of Marketing, S.F. Chamber of Commerce

"John Gumas sees marketing from a businessperson's perspective. Every tip is designed to enhance brand and increase sales. No wonder so many of his ideas resonate with business owners!"
- Susan Armstrong, President and CEO, Armstrong|Shank, Haysville, KS

"John's 'when you can't outspend them, outthink them' strategies are a lesson transcending all Challenger Brands."
- Chris Madsen, President, Mad 4 Marketing, Fort Lauderdale, FL

"John Gumas gets in the trenches to create a true Challenger Brand strategy so you can successfully compete in any market. All of his strategies will increase your brand awareness and bottom line. The bonus is you get to partner with a great guy."
- Timothy J. Malsbury, President, Advertising Concepts, New York, NY

Introduction

I have owned and operated my own advertising agency since 1984. During this time, we have won numerous awards and accolades. But what I am most proud of is the many businesses that we have helped to grow into successful Challenger Brands.

Who's a Challenger Brand? It's any company, regardless of size or industry, that is competing against larger, better-funded competitors.

Challenger Brands must look at marketing in a different way. They never settle for the obvious. They question the status quo. They break conventions. They refuse to be led and always carve out a niche in the market that they can own and defend from anyone. And, most importantly, they understand that they are a Challenger Brand.

In this book, I highlight some of the most effective and successful Challenger Brand strategies from my blog called *Marketing Smart.* Each post is short, sweet and to the point and is designed to provide you with proven insight and strategies that you can apply to your business today.

I hope you enjoy reading Marketing Smart as much as I have enjoyed writing it.

John Gumas

Sign up for John's blog at http://marketingsmart.gumas.com/, follow him on Twitter or write to him directly at jgumas@gumas.com

Or visit marketingsmartbook.com

Contents

SECTION 3—ADVERTISING, MESSAGING & CREATIVITY

SECTION 4—GENERATING RESULTS

SECTION 5—WEBSITE STRATEGY

SECTION 6—ONLINE MARKETING

SECTION 7—TRADESHOWS, PR & OTHER STUFF

SECTION 1—THE BASICS OF SUCCESSFUL MARKETING

Provide yourself with the solid foundation for a powerful business strategy by getting to know as much as you can about your target audience, your competition… and yourself.

Let's Start with the Basics

As marketing professionals, we are always looking for the best ways to brand our companies, cost-effectively reach our customers, develop powerful media plans, etc. We thought it would be valuable to reflect on the most basic marketing strategy of all... how we interact with our customers.

At our agency, we have a very specific description of what our customers mean to us and how they should always be treated. We thought you might want to consider sharing it with your entire staff, and remind them for whom we really work.

A Customer is the most important person ever in this office, either in person or otherwise.

A Customer is not dependent on us. We are dependent on them.

A Customer is not an interruption of our work; they are the purpose of it. We are not doing them a favor by serving them; they are doing us a favor by giving us an opportunity to do so.

A Customer is not an outsider to our business; they are part of it.

A Customer is not a cold statistic, a name on a file or a ledger sheet. They are flesh-and-blood human beings with families, feelings and emotions like our own.

A Customer is not someone to argue with. Nobody ever wins an argument with a customer.

A Customer is a person who brings us their wants. It is our job to fulfill them profitably – for them and for ourselves.

NOTES:

Time for a Marketing Check-up?

It's so easy to get caught up in the day-to-day tactical work that all of us need to do. But every now and then, it's good to stop and take a good view of your marketing efforts from thirty thousand feet.

The following are just a few of the basic questions we feel you should ask yourself before moving forward:

What's your Brand of Distinction?
A brand is a promise to your customers. Whether you intend to or not, all of your marketing contributes toward a brand image in the marketplace. The goal is to control and guide that image into what we call a Brand of Distinction. What is it about your company that is unique only to you? If you have not gone through an exercise to determine your Brand of Distinction, this may be a good time. (See Section 2 of this book for more details on branding.)

Is everyone on the same page?
If someone were to ask all of the key people in your company "why should I do business with you versus your competitors," would everyone answer the same way? And could they answer in less than ten seconds? If you are not on the same page internally, how can you expect to effectively communicate to your marketplace?

Has your positioning strategy changed?
What is your positioning strategy? Has it changed, even slightly, over the past year? And how does your positioning strategy compare to those of your main competitors? If you haven't already done so, create a grid of your main competitors. Where

does each of them fall within that grid? This is a great reality check of where your marketplace is and where it may be heading.

Any new competitors or old competitors doing things differently?

Don't take any one of your competitors for granted. If you have any new competitors, make sure you know everything about them. And be sure that you always monitor your existing competitors to avoid strategic surprises. The more you know about the choices your customers and prospects have, the better you can sell them your products and services.

These are just a few of the most critical touch-points we feel that every marketer should review each year. Obviously, there are many more. It's so easy to stay caught up in the day-to-day frenzy, but take the time to look at the big picture and make sure that all is still on track.

Give Yourself a Marketing Communications Audit

If you haven't done so recently, now is the perfect time to step back and review your overall marketing positioning and messaging strategy to make sure they are still on target. We call it a Marketing Communications Audit.

The following is an outline of the critical components of the Marketing Communications Audit that we take our clients through to determine if they are maximizing their marketing efforts and return on investment:

Internal Interviews – The most valuable information you can gather is from within. Formally interview your key employees to learn from their insight and to inform them of the company's direction and goals.

External Interviews – Formally interview your current clients, past clients and vendors. Ask them what you are doing right and what you can improve upon. And be sure to ask their opinions of your competitors.

Competitive Analysis – Review your key competitors' positioning and messaging strategies. Which competitors pose the greatest threat? Look at their websites, read their collateral materials and experience them for yourself by actually "shopping" them.

Advertising and Creative Style – After you have completed steps one through three, take an objective look at your core advertising strategy, creative messaging and style. Do they match what you have discovered? Do they properly differentiate you from your competitors? Do they say what your customers want to hear?

There are many additional factors that we review when we conduct our Marketing Communications Audits, but these are the most critical. And one last word of caution: Don't try to do this yourself. You are too close to your business to be objective, and your clients and employees may not be completely truthful when speaking directly to you. So consider hiring an outside firm to conduct the audit for you.

Are You Underestimating the Power of a Competitive Analysis?

Successful companies put a lot of time, effort and money into developing a marketing plan. They carefully look at the best ways to maximize their budgets. They dig deep into the demographic and psychographic breakdown of their target audiences. And they scrutinize their outbound efforts to make sure they have the most efficient media mixes.

Most companies have the best intentions when they set out to create a marketing plan. But there is one thing that we consistently see underestimated – and, in many cases, overlooked. That is a thorough, non-biased competitive analysis.

We are not referring to an understanding of your competition from your own perspective. We are referring to a thorough understanding of your competition through your customer's eyes.

Here's how we suggest you format your competitive analysis:

o   Take your top three to five direct competitors in your category. Here's the important part: Be sure to include yourself on that list as well.

o   Now, pretend you are a customer looking for that product or service within your category.

o   Start by doing a little research on each company, just like a real prospect would. Look at each company's website. Look at any printed literature, ads, mailers or other form of communication. Do a keyword Google search. Compare creative styles and messaging. In other words, find everything you can on each company.

o   Next, actually shop each competitor, including yourself. Go through the motions and experience what a prospect would experience. And be sure to keep a non-biased attitude, just like a customer would. At the conclusion, you may be surprised at what you find, especially about yourself. (You may find it more practical to hire someone to do this for you.)

o   Now for the most critical part of this exercise. Ask yourself, truthfully, who would you buy from and why? Warning: The truth may be eye opening.

Don't Forget Your Customers

Nearly 70% of all business lost in America can be directly attributed to ignoring the customer after the sale.

It's an amazing percentage when you think about it. This may be the area where you have the greatest control. We seem to spend all of our time and effort generating new customers. We lure them with catchy ads. We seduce them with slick brochures, websites and other expensive collateral materials. We listen attentively to their problems and help them find creative solutions. We give them a fair price, and then we smile and thank them for their business.

Then... we do nothing. We just ignore them!

There are no hotter or more important new business prospects than your current customers. They liked you and believed in you enough to try you once. Hopefully, they had a satisfactory experience the first time around.

On average, it costs you 80% less to get an existing customer to purchase from you again than it does to generate a new customer.

So why aren't you talking to them? Why aren't you telling them more about the other products and services you can also offer them? Why aren't you asking them to tell you more about what they need?

What you need is a Customer Retention Program.

A Customer Retention Program is critical to the success of any company. Stay in touch with your customers. Reinforce that they made the right decision to work with you in the first place. Let them know what you're doing and the new products or services you have to offer. You just never know what might happen.

What's Your Purchase Cycle?

Before each and every one of us buys something, no matter what it is, we typically go through very specific phases that lead up to our actual purchase. We refer to this process as the Purchase Cycle.

Over the years, we have found that the best way to effectively advertise to our clients' prospects is to first understand the prospects' purchase cycle. Knowing this process beforehand can dramatically enhance our clients' advertising results.

The purchase cycle, as we see it, has five distinct phases. We call them I Don't Know You; I Now Know You; I'm Ready to Give You a Try; I Want More; and I'm Going to Tell a Friend. Here's what each phase means and how your advertising program should be tailored to generate greater results.

Phase 1: I Don't Know You

This first stage is obvious. Your prospect has no idea who you are. Your goal is to get on their radar screen and let them know who you are and what you can do for them. Targeted conventional media (such as print publications, electronic, out of home, etc.), public relations and online media are good tools to build awareness quickly.

Phase 2: I Now Know You

At last, your prospect has an idea of who you are. They've heard your name, so your goal is to get them interested enough to find out more. They are willing to listen if the message is right. Your website, targeted conventional advertising, targeted email, publication partnering and smart promotions work well during this phase. And having a consistent message in all media strengthens and builds your brand.

Phase 3: I'm Ready to Give You a Try
Now, they're seriously thinking about you. They just need that extra little push over the fence to give you a try. Direct mail and email, customer testimonials and strong promotions or trial offers work exceptionally well here.

Phase 4: I Want More
They've tried your product or service. You now want them to buy again. Here's where you need to be sure they know their business is valuable to you. Remember: It's 80% less expensive to get an existing customer to buy again than it is to get a new customer. Customer perks, customer clubs and specialized newsletters/emails all work well. Just stay in front of them with valuable information and make them feel special.

Phase 5: I'm Going to Tell a Friend
This is what every marketer lives for: The Grand Slam of Marketing. During this phase your customers become your salespeople. Their word-of-mouth advertising and referrals become powerful, low-cost sales tools. If you do Phases 1 through 4 correctly, the big payoff comes if you can make it to Phase 5. Try to thank and reward these people as much as you can.

Just knowing about the Five Phases of the Purchase Cycle can dramatically help you in your tactical marketing. Since you most likely have prospects currently within each phase of your cycle, tailoring your message to each of the five phases can be critically important to the success of your marketing program.

Who Is Your Most Important Audience?

Who do you think your company's most important target audience really is? Is it your main prospects? Or maybe it's your existing customers? Both of these answers are close. But your most important audience is typically a group that most companies ignore. It's your employees.

Lots of companies spend a significant percentage of their revenue on marketing. They develop well-thought-out ads designed to get prospects to call. They produce beautiful brochures telling customers all about their great products and services. And they design slick websites that carry their branding and messaging strategies to the masses.

Your employees are your first line of contact with customers. They possess the ability to either make or break your company. Yet how many of us actually spend the time to communicate our marketing and messaging strategy to our employees? Whether they are interacting with a new prospect or an existing customer, your employees must understand your company's message, image and branding strategy. And, more importantly, they must understand how to communicate these messages to your customers and prospects at the point of sale.

Here's a little test to see if your employees understand your company's marketing strategy. Randomly stop a cross section of your employees and ask them the following questions:

1. In one sentence, explain our company's mission. What do our customers buy from us? (If they only say the name of your product, you're in trouble!)
2. Who are our main competitors and what makes us different

from them?

3. What is the most innovative thing this company has done in the past year?

If the answers to these questions are in line with your company's marketing strategy, then you're doing a great job. If not, you need to do some work to get your most important audience on board.

Your Customers: They're Walking Gold Mines of Information

In our hectic day-to-day world of marketing, we sometimes forget the basics of market research and the priceless information it can deliver, not to mention all the money it can save by helping to develop more effective marketing programs.

When most companies start adding market research into their mix, the typical tactics they use to learn basic customer information may include customer satisfaction surveys, focus groups and traffic surveys. We have found that by adding the following market research tactics, companies may glean even more useful information from those walking gold mines we call customers.

Target Audience Profile

Try conducting a survey of existing and past customers to improve your understanding of their key demographics, psychographics and media preferences. This knowledge enhances your creative and messaging efforts, and helps you better focus your media spending.

Trend Forecasting

Some companies go on day after day doing the same old thing. Then one day they walk into the office and say, "What the heck happened?" Don't let this happen to you. Conduct regular studies to learn the latest trends of the marketplace, specifically as these trends relate to your customers. This way, you will be ready to meet their changing needs.

Product Enhancement

To create new products with innovative features and benefits that your customers really want, ask existing customers what they'd like to see from your next generation of products. For example, a homebuilder we know contacted recent customers to learn what their home of the future might provide. Not only did they uncover some very useful information, but those customers were very impressed that they cared enough to ask.

Brand Perception

What do customers really think about your brand? The only way to find out is to talk with them. For example, another homebuilder recently changed its marketing focus when it discovered that the market perceived it to be a safe, traditional homebuilder rather than the creative, high-end builder it actually is.

Market Identification

Knowing which markets are receptive to your specific messages and which ones are not will dramatically increase your results. Recently, a marketing director for a senior home complex discovered that out-of-the-area seniors were more interested in their development than the local seniors. They redirected marketing dollars and significantly increased traffic.

Message Development

Ask your customers and prospects what they find most compelling about your products and services. Then use this information to develop messaging strategies that better resonate with them. The more you know about what they want to hear, the better sales response you'll be able to generate.

Concept Testing

Before spending any money on advertising, test your concepts. This small extra step of making sure your target audience understands what you are trying to say will enable you to be confident that your advertising dollars are being spent wisely.

Customer Satisfaction

It's as important to retain existing customers as it is to generate new customers. Make sure that you interview your customers after the sale and continue to stay in front of them. A recent study shows that by raising your customer retention rates by 5% you can actually increase the value of your average customer by 25% to 100%.

Remember that market research is more than simply conducting surveys and focus groups. It's finding out as much about your customers' perceptions as you can. Just like good advertising, your research should be creative as well.

NOTES:

Do You Know Who Your Best Customers Are?

We've all heard that old saying that 80% of your revenue comes from 20% of your customers. And, for the most part, that old saying is very true. That's why it's so important to work closely with your existing customer base – especially your best customers.

You should always keep existing customers informed of new products or services, or any new opportunities and/or ways to do business with you. At the least, simply communicate with them on a regular basis. This makes for a healthier and more profitable relationship.

But how do you determine which customers are your best customers? We like to use a proprietary rating formula that helps our clients identify which of their customers are actually their best, and most profitable, customers.

This model is called the Gumas Best Customer Profile. This formula weighs specific customer performance activity, such as when they last bought, how frequently they buy, how profitable they are and how easy they are to work with, to create a model of your "real" best customers.

Here's how we do it.

We rate each customer from 1 to 4, with 1 being the lowest score and 4 being the highest. We provide each customer with a score for the following:

(A) When they last bought (1 – 4),
(B) How frequently they buy (1 – 4),

(C) How profitable they are (1 – 4), and

(D) How easy they are to do business with (1 being difficult and 4 being easy).

Add the scores together (A + B + C + D) to get a total for each customer. The highest total scores suggest which of your customers deserve your most attentive service.

Give this simple system a try. It will help you identify those customers who are truly your company's most valued and profitable customers.

How to Find Your Perfect Customer in a Haystack of Prospects

Most companies strive to ensure that every marketing dollar is spent wisely. So how do you deliver on a promise of better targeting, increased return and complete measuring of results? For many of our clients, that answer lies within a process called customer analytics.

An approach that's right for the times.
Customer analytics is a system of calculations that allows companies to leverage valuable customer information already in their possession. It may be the most valuable tool in your marketing arsenal.

Imagine your marketing potential if you could do the following:
- Identify your best, most profitable buying prospects.
- Profile these best prospects so that others like them can be picked out of the crowd.
- Identify customer segments based on their buying habits, unique needs, purchase timing, etc.
- Determine the best opportunities to up-sell each customer segment or increase branding and/or loyalty among your best customers.
- Target prospect segments with custom messages and offers. Then measure the results against a control group to roll out the strategy that generates the best response.
- Enhance your database by adding detailed demographic information, securing a list of additional prospects and more.

Past purchasing behaviors beat any other methodology as a predictor of future purchasing intent.

All of these insights — and more, depending on your specific needs — can be discovered through an analysis of your existing customers and their historical transaction/buying behaviors. Because of its extreme targeting, efficiency and measurability, customer analytics allows you to do more with a smaller budget.

Superior understanding of your customer can drive more effective marketing strategies and create a sustainable competitive advantage.

The customer analytics approach.

The traditional approach to marketing begins with identifying a wide target audience — and targeting that group as a whole. This approach overlooks the multitude of sub-buying groups that, when better understood, can turn a good marketing program into a great one.

Customer analytics data allow companies to reach deeper into the target audience and identify hot, medium and cool prospects before marketing efforts begin. Then initial marketing resources focus only on hot prospects, with a tailored message designed specifically for them. Phase 2 is another targeted campaign aimed at medium prospects with a different message and so on.

The process.

So how does one go about doing this? First of all, partner with a marketing or advertising agency that has database analytics capabilities.

Because past purchasing behavior is the best predictor of future purchasing intent, identify useful customer data within your company's existing database or distribution channel. This would include:

- o Customer names and other identifiers
- o Purchase dates and dollar amounts
- o Purchases by product type or category
- o Other information such as geography, special requests, upgrades, financing, etc.

This data can come from disparate sources and formats. It is then consolidated into a master database, cleansed and made ready for mining and analysis. Proprietary software then makes unlimited queries possible to determine marketing opportunities.

The results can then be merged/purged against secondary industry or demographic data to provide targeted mailing lists, email lists and other specific insights such as messaging tactics.

Track results.
Customer analytics is a great marketing campaign management tool for tracking and measuring the results of various marketing tactics. You can also update the data regularly and re-evaluate to develop the next successful marketing strategy.

It's not for everyone.
Customer analytics can only help companies with access to the right internal customer data. But being armed with this extremely valuable information sets the stage for substantial increases in promotional effectiveness and market share.

NOTES:

Understanding Your Female Audience

Whether you are marketing new homes or consumer electronics, more and more women are now playing a primary role in the decision-making process.

So how do you make sure that you do not alienate women decision-makers in your marketing programs? A series of recent studies outlined some very interesting findings...

As it turns out, women, in general, are "relaters." They see information, products and even themselves in terms of how they relate to others. Typically, women are more comfortable responding to communications that tell relevant stories.

These studies went on to outline that women, unlike men, tell stories in layers. In other words, the richness of the story's details matter as much as the outcome.

So as marketers, what does this mean to us? Many times good advertising takes the form of a story – how your product changed someone's life, how your service makes life easier, etc. Knowing that stories matter as much as the outcome, here are some suggestions you might want to consider for your next advertising campaign that includes women as key decision-makers.

- o Don't start with the ending.
- o The best stories are emotionally charged – so make sure your marketing is too.
- o Don't just cut to the facts – take time to tell the story.
- o Let your reader feel the impact of the relationships.
- o Make it matter.

Thoroughly understanding your target audience is essential to the success of your marketing and advertising campaigns. The more you know about who the real buyer is, the more relevant, and successful, your advertising campaign will be.

It's Not About You

We work with many different types of companies. All of them feel that they understand their customers, their market and their unique positioning. But time and time again, we see that many of them make a very common, and expensive, marketing assumption.

When it comes to marketing your company, product or service, remember this… it's not about you. It never was about you. And it will never be about you.

No matter how well you think you know your target audience, make a conscious effort to remove yourself from the messaging and advertising. It doesn't matter that your ad speaks to you personally. It doesn't matter that you like the colors. It doesn't matter that it motivates you. It only matters how it appears to your target audience.

Who cares what you like?
It's so easy for all of us to put personal likes and dislikes into our advertising and messaging decisions. Be honest now. How much of your advertising and messaging decisions do you base on what you personally like? The reality is, it doesn't matter if you like it or not. The only thing that matters is whether your target audience will be motivated to buy.

So what's a marketer to do? Here's how we approach it.

- o   Know your audience inside and out.
- o   Don't fall into the trap of thinking you know your target market well enough. Even if you fall within the target audience, you still don't know them. You only know

yourself. Many people feel that their opinions and beliefs mirror their peers'. That's not typically the case. Don't base decisions as large as this on your gut feeling alone.

Do the market research. Talk to your customers. Talk to your sales people. Answer the phones every now and then and speak directly to your prospects. Do everything you can to get into the shoes of your prospective customers. That's the best way to be sure that your advertising is speaking to the right people.

Show Them the Benefits

All well-written marketing materials emphasize features. Sure, it's nice to know "the what" of a product or service, but your customers are mostly interested in "the why" of your products.

When your marketing materials and ads sell the features, you leave the audience to extrapolate "the why" on their own. But it can be dangerous to leave your audience to figure out or assume to know the benefits of your products on their own.

Never stop at the features. Continue directly to the benefits and help your audience understand why they need or want the benefits your product has to offer.

Here are some examples of turning "the what" into "the why."

Feature: It's long lasting.
Benefit: This atomic flashlight will outlive you – even if you're only four years old.

Feature: It's faster.
Benefit: You'll never again wait for another web page to load while you stare at a blank screen.

Feature: It will organize all of your financial records.
Benefit: Lack of receipts and records cost the average American $538 in tax deductions a year. Do you want to lose $538 again this year?

Feature: We're trustworthy.
Benefit: The kind of financial advice you'd want for your rich uncle.

Features are nice, but the benefit is where the emotional tug exists. And it's with that emotional tug that the consumer will find motivation to buy from you.

Finally, you don't always have to use words to describe the benefit. Sometimes your visual can make the point with as much, if not more, emotional strength.

Going in for the Kill

Baron Von Richthofen, also known as the Red Baron, was considered one of the great aces of World War I. But what made him so great? A major tactic in his strategy was to always finish off his opponent and "go in for the kill."

The Baron would have made a great marketing professional. When it comes to marketing tactics, many companies don't carry all the way through with their marketing programs. They typically fall just short of conclusion. And, unlike the Baron, they don't go in for the kill.

So what do we mean by not going in for the kill? The following are just some of the many examples we see on a regular basis:

o   Sending out direct mail and never following up.
o   Running print ads without a strong call-to-action.
o   Giving up on an interested prospect after just a couple of calls.
o   After a networking event, not following up with the new contacts in a timely manner.
o   Most leads generated at a tradeshow are either followed up with too late or, even worse, are never followed up with at all.

The typical marketer makes it a priority to chase after new business prospects, and when they finally get close, they either stop or put it off for so long that the prospect has lost interest or, dare we say, purchased from a competitor. This is only one of many examples we see regularly, but the point here is if you want marketing to work at its highest level, you have to go in for the kill.

Why does this happen? The most common reason we see is that there is no secondary plan in place to deal with the low-level tactics. What happens once someone responds? When strategic plans are created, they usually outline top-level strategy. Plans do not typically have a secondary plan that goes into this low-level "how are we going to close the business" tactical detail. Yet this stage of the prospect courtship may be the most crucial stage of all. So a prospect that you've worked so hard to identify and cultivate simply falls off your radar screen because you didn't have a plan in place designed to go in for the kill.

So what do we suggest? Never execute any plan until you know exactly how you're going to finish it off. Always have the next steps figured out before you execute. Take a close look at your marketing plans to see if they do in fact go in for the kill. If not, it's most likely costing you in lost opportunity revenue.

Driving Consumers to Purchase

A recent study set out to find what marketing tactics motivated consumers to move from "considering a purchase" to actually "making a purchase." The results of the study are eye opening and worthy of our close attention as we all plan our next marketing campaign.

The study results are as follows:

(Note: Respondents could pick more than one influencer, so the total is more than 100%.)

1. Free sample 87.2%
2. Referral from a friend 48.5%
3. Free premium 29.4%
4. Advertising 27.2%
5. Chance to win instant major prize 16.7%
6. Packaging 10.2%
7. Direct mail 5.0%
8. Presence around town 4.6%
9. Collateral 2.4%

The results raise the question – how can you incorporate one of these tactics into your next marketing campaign to increase your results?

NOTES:

Planning for Greater Success

One of the main goals of any advertising plan should be to maximize your potential return on investment. Here is a tip to consider.

Let's say your budget allows you to purchase a full-page, full-color ad in six different publications. Instead of choosing six publications, consider only advertising in the top three publications. With the balance of the money, try including both conventional direct mail and electronic mail targeting the exact same audience.

By hitting a smaller, targeted group using multiple advertising vehicles simultaneously, in this case print, direct mail and email campaigns, you will make a bigger impact with the same ad dollars.

Also don't forget to seek merchandising credits from your chosen publications for use in purchasing names from their database for your follow-up direct mail and e-vertising efforts. The names from these databases are almost always fresher than your internal or other purchased databases due to the requirements for frequent audits. They also guarantee that your direct mail and email campaigns will reach the same target as your print ads.

As long as you execute this strategy by utilizing the proper reach and frequency models, you should see a bigger return on your advertising investment.

NOTES:

Don't Throw Out the Baby with the Bath Water

We see it happen all too often: A marketer tries a specific tactic a couple of times, say a newspaper or magazine ad. Or they may even be diligent and try it many times. But they just don't get the response they expect. So they decide newspaper or magazine advertising doesn't work.

Sometimes, it might not be the tactic at all. Think of your marketing as the driver in a car. And think of your marketing tactics as the engine of that car. Once behind the wheel, if you know where you want to go and how to get there, your marketing tactics will help you get there quickly and efficiently. But if you're driving without directions or a map, then it doesn't matter how finely tuned your engine is or how many horses it has.

Think of a marketing plan as that map. Without an effective marketing strategy, you'll never achieve the results you want, no matter how much time and money you spend (or how many horses you have under the hood).

A marketing plan can take the shape of an overall marketing program or it can be broken into a tactic-specific plan. For example, a high-profile radio ad campaign won't help you grow your business unless it includes a timely message that will attract the specific needs of your target customer. An article written about you in the newspaper or trade press can bring in new clients or be a worthless conversation piece. Outbound email messages can either end up in your prospects' delete bins, or they can prompt them to contact you.

So what are the fundamental principles of a sound marketing

plan? The following are some of the <u>basic elements</u> we include in our marketing strategies. Your particular situation will always prompt even more specific elements.

1. **Target Audience.** The most basic of all elements, but it is amazing how many marketers take this information for granted. Truly know who your customers are (both demographically and psychographically) and why they buy.

2. **Key Competition.** Always know every purchase option your prospect has and what your competitors are saying to attract your prospect so you can offer something better or different.

3. **Key Benefits.** Why is your product, service or offering better than the competition and how does this relate directly to the needs of your target?

4. **Objective.** Define your success. What does this marketing plan or tactic have to do or deliver to be successful?

5. **Strategy.** After you've answered items one through four above, what needs to be done to make your definition of success a reality?

Before you begin any marketing tactic, be sure you know what success needs to look like. And before you decide a particular tactic doesn't work, make sure that the strategy was a sound one.

Why Advertising Campaigns Fail

Advertising by nature is extremely subjective. As a result, what seems to be a great advertising idea can turn out to be a failure. The following are five of the most common reasons why advertising campaigns fail.

Stretching your budget too far.
Understand your budget and what is realistic. We consistently see clients trying to stretch their budgets to do more than the budget will allow. Try not to spread your media buy or marketing tactics so thin that you can't afford to repeat them liberally. It's always better to do fewer things more often.

Got to have it now.
There always seems to be this need for instant gratification. Effective marketing is about creating mind share. And you don't earn that instantaneously. It is a process and part of a long-term plan. On average, you need to create anywhere between six and fifteen impressions before your prospect will seriously notice you. (See also "Are You Giving Up Too Quickly on Your Advertising?" in Section 3.)

Believing that you are a focus group of one.
Many marketers believe that their perception is unbiased and accurate. When you're on the inside looking out, it is very difficult to be objective about your own company. It is the perception of your customers and prospects that counts. Engage in a non-biased process to discover the truth of what your customers and prospects think and want versus what you think. (See "Your Customers: They're Walking Gold Mines of Information" earlier in this section.)

Not backing up your promises.

Be wary of using hype and boastful language, such as "we have the lowest prices," "best service" or "highest quality." Your promises have to be believable. If you overdo it, your customers will know. And if they don't believe you, they won't respond.

Creative-heavy and strategy-light.

We've all seen those TV commercials and print ads that are very clever, but we can't remember the brand name they are supposed to be promoting. Remember that your advertising can't just be creative; it also has to be on strategy. Entertaining your audience is good, but winning their business is better.

Over the years, we have turned many of our clients' advertising programs from failures to successes simply by watching for and correcting these types of mistakes. As obvious as the above seems, it is very easy for marketers to get caught up in any one of them. Take a few minutes to examine your current advertising to see if you are guilty of any of these common mistakes.

The Five Most Overlooked Mistakes in Marketing

The marketing and promotion of any product or service can be challenging. The objective should be to have your marketing budget generate the greatest possible return on your investment. Sounds simple enough. So then why do many marketing plans fail to achieve this critical objective?

To help guide you down the right path, we have compiled a list of the top five less obvious marketing mistakes we see companies make most often.

#1: "Who Cares" Copy

Take a look at all of your marketing materials – brochures, direct mail, website, print advertising, collateral materials. How many times do they say "our," "us" or "we"?

The problem with most copy is that it is "who cares" copy. In other words, if the copy is riddled with "our," "us" and "we," then it's all about you. Switch the focus of your copy to the reader by changing the copy into "you," "your" or "yours" copy. This simple adjustment has a much better chance of pulling your reader in.

Too many companies focus on themselves rather than the needs and wants of their prospective customers. Features are about you; benefits are about your prospective customer. Benefits are the compelling advantages your product or service provides. So when creating advertising campaigns and collateral materials, always lead with your most compelling benefits and then support those benefits with the features. Features don't sell; benefits directed to your reader do.

#2: Your Visuals Are Obvious and Not Compelling

We see it all the time – the predictable stock photo, or worse, the even more predictable (and often cheesy) clip art. These visuals are so obvious that no one pays attention. And very often, they reflect a poor image of your company or product.

Visuals are very critical components of your marketing messages. This is not the place to get cheap or lazy. This is the place to be creative and shine.

#3: Not Enough Direct Response Advertising

Brand advertising tells your target audience about your company, products and services. Direct response advertising provokes a response. Successful advertising does both.

Always include a strong call-to-action. Typically, prospects will respond if there is a compelling reason to do so. Get creative, and be sure to create a sense of urgency – you want to hear from your target immediately. (See Section 4 for tips on making your direct response advertising successful.)

#4: Type That's Too Hard to Read

You can write the most compelling copy possible, but if your final type is too hard to read, it will simply die on the page. Take a look at all of your marketing materials. Are you breaking any of the following rules?

o   type smaller than 10-point
o   more than two lines of centered type
o   type that's justified on both sides
o   more than three lines of reverse type
o   sentences longer than 15 words
o   paragraph blocks that are more than six lines long

If you answered yes to any of the above, chances are you are losing readers. We do recognize that there are exceptions to the above rules, but for the most part, if you want people to read your text, make it clear.

#5: Buying the Cheapest Media, Not the Best Media
Do you base your media decisions on the lowest price media available? If you were to do a detailed analysis, you'd probably discover that you're not saving money at all. You're probably losing opportunities to effectively market your company. And, you may be hurting your overall brand image.

Cheap media is cheap for a reason. You should buy media that best delivers your target audience, offers the right association for your brand and is respected within your market niche. Then, to be sure, you should test everything you do, so that you know what works and what doesn't.

Watch out for these less obvious but very common marketing mistakes. Take a close look at your marketing programs and see how many you are making. If you correct them, we promise you will see a difference in your marketing results.

NOTES:

The Most Common Marketing Mistakes

The marketing and promotion of any product or service is a challenge. What's the best way to market my company? What strategies should I use? How do I best allocate my budget to get the greatest impact and return?

We've compiled a list of five of the most common mistakes companies make when marketing their products and services.

Mistake #1 – Creating Institutional, Instead of Direct Response, Advertising

Successful direct response advertising is the process of providing your target audience with a compelling reason to respond coupled with a strong call-to-action. That call-to-action could be as simple as "call us," "visit our website" or "get a free something." Typically, prospects will respond if there is a compelling reason to do so. In everything you do, be sure to give them an offer they can't refuse. And be sure to create a sense of urgency – you want to hear from your target immediately.

Mistake #2 – Not Having a USP

A Unique Selling Proposition, or USP, is what sets you apart from your competition. Without one, you are just another company out there. What makes you different from your competitors? What benefit do you offer that your competitors don't? Some companies actually make their name part of their USP, such as Best Buy, Budget Car Rental or Bob's All Natural Foods. Define your USP and stick to it.

Mistake #3 – Failure to Address Your Customers' Needs

Successful companies always ask their prospects and customers what they want. They don't assume. The only reason someone does business with you is to fulfill a need or solve a problem. You must find out what these needs and desires are, and then fulfill them better than any of your competitors.

Mistake #4 – Talking Features and Not Benefits

Try not to focus on your company, product or service but rather the wants and needs of your target audience. All your prospect cares about is "what's in it for me?" In promotional material, emphasize the benefits and then support those benefits with the product or service's features.

Mistake #5 – Not Having a Back-end

Many companies put 100% of their advertising focus toward generating new customers. Typically, of those new prospects who respond, a very small percentage buy. A strong back-end marketing program can help you close a larger percentage of these prospects over time. You should develop a separate program that exclusively targets these prospects. A strong back-end is a very low-cost way to dramatically increase sales.

The Deadly Sins of Marketing

As we all know, there are many ways your marketing plan can go wrong. So what can you do to make sure that your marketing efforts are generating the greatest exposure and return on investment?

Instead of focusing on the many possible strategies a good marketing plan must include, we've outlined the most common mistakes that companies make. If you simply avoid these common pitfalls, you should enjoy a considerable difference in your marketing and advertising returns:

1. Lack of marketing focus – Do you know who you are? Do you know what makes you different from your competition? But most importantly, do your customers and prospects know? Don't try to be everything to everyone. Identify what makes you unique, keep that message simple and stick to it.

2. Overlooking testing and research – How did that last ad pull for you? Did you decide to use that creative tactic because that's what your research told you? If you want to gamble, go to Las Vegas. If you want a return on your marketing dollars, conduct some targeted research.

3. Lack of consistent image – If you have a smaller ad budget than your larger competitors, creating a recognizable image in the marketplace is challenging. To accomplish this, you must be religiously consistent in everything you do. That includes your look, style, messaging, media and call-to-action. The more you waver from consistency, the less effectiveness you will achieve.

4. Overlooking existing customers – You'll find us often citing this statistic because of its importance: On average, getting an existing customer to buy something else from you or to refer you to new business is 80% more likely than generating a new customer. Whether it's formal or informal, every company should have a program in place that keeps you in front of your existing customers.

5. Creating brand advertising instead of direct response advertising – Brand advertising tells your target audience about your company, products and services. Direct response advertising does the same thing, but, as the name implies, it invokes a response. Your advertising should always include a strong call-to-action that provides your prospects with a compelling reason to respond now, not later.

Are you guilty of at least one of these? If not, congratulations. If so, now's a good time to redirect your marketing and advertising efforts.

Marketing in an Economic Downturn

Marketing through an economic downturn can be challenging. Do you cut marketing programs to save money? How do you increase sales and maximize your activity during these challenging times? Here are some ideas to think about.

An economic slowdown doesn't mean you should abandon your marketing plans. It means you need to be savvy enough to take advantage of the current business climate.

Keep in mind that most of your competitors are running scared. Smart marketers are gearing up activity to take advantage of a quieter marketplace. This means you can garner more attention for your message and gain market share and market awareness.

This does not mean spending money foolishly. A good strategy during these times is to focus on your existing customer base, those who already know and trust you. It's not a time for a splashy image campaign. Demonstrate value. Demonstrate customer awareness. Demonstrate stability.

Studies show that companies that maintain or increase marketing and sales efforts not only weather a recession much better than their competitors, but they come out of the downturn faster and with greater gains in market share, sales and profits.

Marketing is like pushing a huge boulder. It's the momentum that keeps things going. Once you stop, it's very hard (and expensive) to get rolling again.

SECTION 2—BRAND DEVELOPMENT

Your success depends on discovering the true essence of your company and what you can offer your customers that no one else can. This section will help you develop an identity that will position you to stand head and shoulders above your competition.

What Is Branding and Why Is It So Important for Your Company?

So, what's this thing called "branding" that everyone talks about? Branding is one of those terms that if you ask ten different marketing experts to define it, you'll get ten different answers. The one consistent point you will hear is how important a coordinated branding program is to your company's success.

It's all about your customers' perception.

Branding can become a strategic and powerful asset for any company. Branding has nothing to do with how *you* perceive your company, its products and services. It has everything to do with how *your customers and prospects* perceive your company, its products and services.

Branding is many things, but mainly it is a process of positively differentiating yourself from your competition and making sure your target audience knows why you're different. Your target audience must be made to know what they can expect when doing business with you. In a nutshell, your brand is the intangible component of your company that gives customers a compelling reason to do business with you instead of your competition.

The power of branding.

A properly developed brand is a powerful asset. Brands don't just happen; they are carefully and strategically created. What comes to mind when you think of BMW automobiles, McDonald's restaurants or Owens-Corning insulation? If the relentless branding efforts by these companies have paid off, these brands should create a comfort level and an understanding of what you can expect when doing business with them.

So how do you build a brand?

Unless you have a huge marketing budget to undertake a major-league branding campaign, like the sample companies outlined above, you'll need to take a realistic, common-sense approach to branding your company. Consider an approach that uses your existing marketing promotions, efforts and dollars to continuously contribute to your overall branding effort.

Corporate identity.

Let's get the most basic requirement out of the way first. All of the materials and messaging your company produces and distributes must be consistent. This includes your company and product logos, ads, website, public relations, online marketing, brochures and other collateral materials and anything else that delivers your message to your targeted market.

From a visual perspective, there should be a distinctive creative style to everything you create. Your messaging must always be simple to understand, unique and consistent.

Corporate philosophy.

Here's where it gets a little deeper. Developing a true brand is much more than creating ads, brochures and websites with a similar look and message. Branding is a comprehensive system of developing a corporate philosophy that translates into everything you do.

What's it like to do business with your company? From the moment a customer calls, walks into your retail location or encounters a salesperson somewhere within the channel, the building of your brand is at work. You cannot and should not leave this to chance. To create a powerful brand, you must incorporate every aspect of your business process into the development of your brand.

For example, you want to brand yourself as a customer service organization, yet when someone calls your company, they get an impersonal voice mail system. How do you think this may affect your overall brand?

Take a close look at every aspect of your business as it relates to your marketing and advertising functions. The development of a brand does not happen overnight. It is an ongoing process in which you are establishing, maintaining and enhancing your company's image, recognition, trust and comfort level among your customers and prospects at every point of contact.

Build a trusted brand and it will pay huge dividends for you.

NOTES:

Have You Discovered Your Real Brand of Distinction?

Every company has a unique brand of distinction. It lives deep down in the soul of your organization. It is the collective sum of all the history, emotions, thoughts and stereotypes that exist about your company. For marketing purposes, it is simply that core value, promise or position that makes your company different in the eyes of the customer.

But, sadly enough, most companies never take the time to discover what theirs truly is. While most executives may have an understanding of why their company is unique, the stumbling point comes when they try to verbalize this story to their customers, prospects and even their own employees.

Some companies fail by using common or bland language and making vague promises that do not set them apart. They become lost in the crowd. For example, what do the following taglines say about these company brands?

- o Our quality is second to none
- o Your success is our success
- o Customer service is our pleasure
- o Great value for your dollar

The answer is... not much. In fact, these are very common branding taglines used by many companies today. In the end, these are simply promises every business should be making to its customers, regardless of its brand. These generic phrases certainly don't describe a brand of distinction because there is nothing unique about them.

So, what's a marketer to do? Start by taking a close, hard look at your existing brand essence and be brutally honest with yourself. What about your company is unique among your main competitors? Is it a position that you truly own? Is it one that you can easily defend against your competitors?

A powerful brand essence is the foundation upon which all successful marketing is built. Discover a unique brand of distinction and watch your company grow.

Don't Fall Into the Branding Trap

We've talked about branding and how important it is to the success of any organization. But do you know the difference between branding and brand development? This is where many organizations make a potentially fatal mistake and fall into the branding trap.

Here's the critical difference: Brand development is the discovery process that identifies your brand's unique distinction in the marketplace. Branding is the tactical elements utilized to take that distinction to market.

A brand is not a slogan, a typeface, a logo or a color. These are branding tactics. Simply put, a brand is a unique claim of distinction made consistently over time (Coke, Nike, Mercedes, HP). This claim is what truly separates you from all of your competitors. Without this unique claim of distinction, your company becomes indistinguishable and your product or service offering may be on its way to becoming simply a commodity.

A strong brand carries such a unique claim of distinction that no competitor can ever touch it. Do you remember the Maytag Repairman? Maytag did such a powerful job of identifying and owning the dependability category that no competitor could ever enter that category successfully.

So why go through all of this trouble? Simple. Customers perceive a strong, properly targeted brand to be of higher quality, to offer greater reliability and to provide far better value. For example, consider these statistics:

- The number one brand has a 10% price premium over the number two brand, and a 40% price premium over a "non-branded" product.
- Brands generate customer loyalty. These repeat and referral sales can reduce your cost-of-sales by up to 90%.
- Strong brands build internal company loyalty and pride.

The power of identifying your brand's unique distinction is critical. If you have gone through this discovery process already and have discovered your brand's unique distinction, then you are on the right path for growth and success. If you have not already undergone this very informative process then we highly recommend doing so.

Do You Have a Great Brand Name?

Most every company has a brand name. A brand separates Company X from Company Y. It's the name that customers and prospects know and remember. So logic would tell you that your brand name is a very critical part of your positioning, your image and your overall success.

But what makes a great brand name? We have worked with many clients over the years helping them name new companies, new products and product lines. We feel a great brand name must not only engage the target, but persuade them (either consciously or subconsciously) to want to do business with you.

The following are some of the basics that we start with when we undertake a naming project:

It must communicate the essence of the brand.
All names create their own intrinsic meaning. They can be rational and descriptive (such as Discount Building Supply) or more emotional and imaginative (such as Yahoo). In either case, every name creates a meaning and ultimate brand image to your target. We believe your brand name should communicate your brand's strategy and its essence. Whatever name you settle on, it must communicate the right brand image to your target.

It must be easy to say.
Just look around you at some of the brand names you see in your industry and your day-to-day life. Some brand names are easy to say and roll right off your tongue. These brands typically give you a good feeling about the company. A strong brand name is not only easy to say, but everyone should be able to pronounce it (and spell it) the same way.

It must fit within a naming system.
This is referred to as nomenclature. Simply put, it means having a naming system that will allow you to grow and add new products or services that also fit logically within your brand. A great example of this is what Apple Computer did with its iMac, iPod, iPhoto, iPad, etc. They created a powerful naming system that became a critical component of its brand success.

It must be unique to you.
As you build your brand, be sure that you protect it. Your brand name is a huge investment. It is one of your main differentiators in the marketplace, separating your products and services from your competitors. Not only should your brand name be ownable, but your brand essence should be as well.

As you can see, we believe the naming of a company, product or service is much more than coming up with a name. It is a process that every organization should take very seriously. We also believe it should be part of a larger process of identifying and differentiating one of your most powerful potential assets – your brand essence.

Is Your Brand Imploding?

We have written about how to identify your unique brand essence. We've also written about how you develop a brand of distinction. And we've written about how you effectively develop these into a powerful branding program.

But recently we were brought in to help a company figure out why their brand was losing its effectiveness in the market. What we discovered was very interesting. Their brand was actually imploding.

At Gumas, we are always preaching that a brand is much more than a logo or a tagline. Your true brand is your company's promise. It is the one thing that makes you different. Most companies we speak with understand the power of creating the right brand. But here's where they seem to fall short – ensuring that all of their employees understand the company's brand essence and breathe life into it each and every day.

Here's what we recommend:

Involve all employees – Ask their opinions on how to bring your brand to life, and make sure you keep them informed on all branding activity and goals.

Make it real – Get all employees involved. Let them know how they can deliver the brand to your customers and then reward their efforts.

Show them why it matters – Help them understand the importance of branding. Create measurable benchmarks that can be worked towards and celebrated.

Lead by example – If you bend your own branding rules then so will the rest of your team.

The more conscious you are of helping all of your employees understand and value your brand, the more powerful your brand will become. Don't let your branding efforts implode. Branding elevates to a completely different level when your entire team marches in unison.

What's in a Tagline?

Anyone who has ever gone through the experience of developing a company tagline knows just how difficult this process can be. How do you deliver a memorable message in a single, short sentence?

To develop an effective tagline, you must start by spending some time getting to the core of what your business is all about. Focus on not only what you do, but also how and why you do it. The How and Why of your business is typically your point of differentiation.

Be bold. A tagline should not be humble. Use powerful words that connote emotions beyond the word's definition. This is a daunting task. We typically take clients through an all-day exercise just to identify the message before we even start crafting the phrase. Developing a company tagline is not for the faint of heart.

Here are some tagline dos and don'ts:

o   It should be no longer that seven words. But remember: the shorter the tagline, the better.

o   If your company name is not descriptive of what you do, then your tagline should be.

o   It must be used consistently, on all marketing materials, for a minimum of three to five years.

o   It must be unique to your business. It cannot describe any of your competitors.

o   It avoids using trite or predictable words like "consumer-driven" or "friendly."

o   It should be true. It should be the soul of who your company already is or is working to be.

Five Keys to Creating a Powerful Company Tagline

Just do it. Breakfast of Champions. We try harder.

What do these taglines have in common? They are all examples of memorable taglines that brilliantly positioned their company's brand and helped propel them to new heights.

So what is a tagline? A tagline is a branding message. It positions your company in the market and makes a promise of what your brand is or what it will deliver. The creation of a tagline is a critical undertaking for any company and could mean the difference between status quo and greatness.

So how do you create a powerful tagline that could help propel your company to new heights? The following is the Gumas checklist that we put together when we are developing new taglines for our clients.

1. Is it impactful?
A powerful tagline must be unique, original and bold. It must deliver a promise or set a tone for your brand. And it must do it quickly; we suggest in no more than six or seven words.

2. Does it have sticking power?
In other words, is it memorable? Your tagline must be relevant and has to resonate in the minds of your customers and prospects.

3. Is it easy to say?
If it's hard to say, no one will say it. Not only must it roll off the tongue but it should be simple.

4. Does it communicate your brand benefit?
Not benefits but the single most powerful benefit of your brand – what we call your "brand essence."

5. Does it move you forward?
A strong tagline not only reflects your brand's "here and now" but it should also reflect your future strategic direction.

Take a close look at your current tagline. Now compare it to your brand essence and ask yourself our five questions for creating a powerful company tagline. If it passes your test, congratulations. If it falls short, you have some work to do. And if you don't have a tagline, then you should seriously consider creating one.

NOTES:

SECTION 3—ADVERTISING, MESSAGING & CREATIVITY

You may offer the best product or service in the world, but if your target audience doesn't know about it, you're not going to do very good business. We're going to explore proven strategies that can make the most of this important investment in your success, from what to say to how to say it to how often to say it.

What Makes an Effective Ad?

Ever wonder why some print ads generate an enormous response, while others seem to just fall flat on their faces? Before you can create an effective ad, you must first understand the anatomy of an ad and what it needs to accomplish.

Development of effective ads starts with a clear understanding of your target audience, your competition and the media in which the ad is running. It also takes a clear understanding of why your target audience will buy from you. Armed with this information, you are ready to create impactful advertising. Here are just a few of the most critical design factors.

Grab their attention.
An effective print ad must communicate a simple-to-understand message. To do this, it should have a powerful headline of no more than seven to nine words, and/or an image that captures the attention of the reader. The ad must get this message across in about two to five seconds, because that's how fast the average person flips through a typical publication.

Pull them into the ad.
So you've grabbed the reader's attention. Now what? At this point in the process, the average reader will give you another five to fifteen seconds of their valuable time to hear your story. The body copy needs to tell your story quickly, outlining only those specific benefits that are the most important to the reader, not you. Be sure to make your story interesting, believable and credible, or you will lose the reader's interest. It's okay to use subheads and bullet points. A good rule of thumb is the more expensive your product is, the more copy your prospect is willing to read.

Tell them to do something.

If a reader has focused on your ad this long, then chances are they believe that you have something they want or need. Don't leave them now. Tell them what you want them to do – tell them to call your toll-free number to receive your special offer, or tell them to go to your website to get a free White Paper. Tell them to do something that allows you to capture their names and bring the desired relationship to the next level. Be sure that your offer is credible and consistent with your ad message and is strong enough to get the reader to respond.

Before you create any ad, try to understand the process your reader will go through and what will get them to buy. Once you have a true understanding of this process and can design advertising to attract your target, you should see a measurable difference in your response.

It's All About How You Say It

Developing the proper marketing mix is critical to the success of any advertising program. Newspaper and magazine, television, radio, Internet, direct mail and outdoor advertising can all be effective media for delivering your message to your target audience. But if your message doesn't move your prospects, your advertising is destined for failure. When crafted right, your creative message can deliver incredible results, no matter which vehicles you use.

So what does "crafted right" mean? Let's outline the critical elements of successful messaging and what you can do to dramatically increase your advertising response. You must first attract the prospect's attention, then provoke their interest, create a desire for what you are selling and, finally, induce a specific action.

(1) Attract Attention

If you can't attract the attention of your prospects, it really doesn't matter what you have to tell them in your advertising because they'll never get far enough to read or hear it. Make sure you know what your customers want. Just think about the most important benefit you have to offer, as it pertains to your prospects, and focus on that. And remember that this benefit must be pertinent to what your prospects really want, not what you think your prospects *might* want. Do your homework because if you get this one wrong, chances are your advertising won't work.

In print, most attention is generated in the headline. Words alone can attract the prospect's attention. But, when you combine a powerful headline with an eye-popping visual, your ad has the makings of success.

Be careful not to get too clever. Get right to the point, and try to make your headline no longer than seven words.

(2) Provoke Their Interest

Now that you've captured the prospect's interest, you must now hold that interest with information that is important to your prospect.

The use of simple images and/or photos that support your message is very critical. They help you get your message across faster. When using photos, try to include captions whenever possible. Captions tend to get read more often, so make sure the captions are equally relevant and powerful.

Short, simple sentences keep your prospect's interest best, as does copy that's believable and presented in everyday language. Prospects tend to tune out clichés such as "we are committed to providing the ultimate in service and quality." Instead, you can make this same point by saying "we have hundreds of satisfied customers, and we stand behind each one of them with the best warranty in the industry."

(3) Create Desire

This is where you must excite the prospects. During this third phase, you must give prospects an opportunity to imagine what it would be like if they owned your product.

If your company sells homes, create the visual benefits and build their desire to live in one of your beautifully crafted homes. Paint a picture of what it would be like for them and their family – sitting in front of the gorgeous stone fireplace, taking long walks in the nearby park, relaxing in the Jacuzzi tub after a long day.

The key to building desire is to focus on benefits, not features. A feature tells the prospects what the product has. Benefits, on the other hand, tell your prospects how that feature improves their lives.

(4) Induce Action

Now that you've got your prospect's attention and interest, the final phase may be the most important. Be sure to tell them what you want them to do and when you want them to do it. But it's not good enough to say "buy now" or "come by and see us today." You must give them a compelling reason to do so.

An effective call-to-action must be clear and direct. In addition, make sure that it's relevant to the needs of your prospects, consistent with your product and/or brand, and, most importantly, make sure it provides a sense of urgency for the prospects to respond now.

Now that you have an understanding of the basic elements of effective advertising, you'll be able to craft a message that not only grabs your target audience's attention but also compels them to do business with you. Good luck!

NOTES:

But Why?

Those of you who have children can truly relate to the mind-numbing effect of the word "why," especially when asked over and over again. And yet, that same word is one of marketing's most powerful triggers.

Most people fill their marketing vehicles with the "what" when it comes to selling their products or services – details, facts, figures. It is usually what they are most proud of, the features of their wares. It's also what they understand best. They can rattle off the cool colors or the precise number of GHz or how much titanium is in their new gizmo.

But those "whats" are meaningless to the potential customer without the "why." Why would anyone pay extra for that midnight blue gadget? Why is the 3.0 GHz processor machine better than the perfectly fine computer I currently own? How will my life change if I buy that new titanium gizmo? Once a customer understands the "why," then they can create their own motivation to buy. Stimulating the "why" in the customer's mind is the basic psychology of the sale and at the core of successful marketing and advertising.

Instead of telling them about the details, facts and figures, tell them how that new midnight blue gadget will make them look slimmer. Show them how that new 3.0 GHz computer will keep them from missing deadlines. Promise how that new gizmo will give them more time to spend with their family. Look deep to discover the "whys" behind the facts that will motivate someone to go out and buy your products and services.

Now is a good time to evaluate all of your current marketing tools. Do they simply communicate a list of "what" facts or do they motivate through the emotional "whys"? No matter how mind numbing it threatens to be, keep asking yourself "why" until you discover the real emotion behind your product or service. Then make sure you spotlight the real buying motivation in everything you do.

Six Tips to Make Your Messages Sticky

When it comes to advertising campaigns, some you forget as soon as you see them and others you can never forget. The ideas that you never forget are sometimes referred to as "sticky ideas," simply because they stick with you over time.

There's a process that can be used to craft ideas that will "stick" with your intended audiences. Here are the key elements:

1. Keep it simple. It's hard to make ideas stick in our chaotic environment. Strip your idea down to its most critical essence.

2. Do the unexpected. Break an obvious pattern. Communicate your message in a way that surprises your audience.

3. Get to the point. Abstraction makes it harder to understand an idea and to remember it. Be specific and get to the point.

4. Establish credibility. Earn trust by talking the talk. Show your expertise. Details matter.

5. Appeal to the emotions. Appeal to your audience's self-interest, but also appeal to their identities – not just who they are, but who they want to be.

6. Tell your story. Stories are the culmination of the other five criteria outlined above. Weave a simple and credible story. Use the juxtaposition of concrete facts plus the unexpected to trigger an emotional response.

The next time you need to make your advertising ideas stand out and become "sticky," try this system. It really works.

NOTES:

The Ten Most Powerful Words in Advertising

Mark Twain once said "the difference between using the right word and almost the right word is the difference between a lightning bug and lightning." In advertising, the idea is very similar. Imagine if you could use words in your advertising that could change your advertising from good to great!

There have been numerous studies conducted over the years on this subject. Each one was designed to find those words believed to be the most persuasive in advertising. We thought it would be interesting to compare those studies to determine which words consistently made it to the top of the lists. Then we refined the lists to include those words that we have found to be the most persuasive during the past 25 years that we have been creating advertising campaigns.

The result is the following list of what we feel may be The Ten Most Powerful Words in Advertising*:

1. **NEW** – Having something new and knowing something is new has incredible intrinsic value.

2. **GUARANTEED** – We are all reluctant to try something new because of the risk. Take away that risk by guaranteeing a sure thing.

3. **PROVEN** – Another no-risk word that assures your target audience that your product has already been tested by others.

4. **RESULTS** – This is the bottom line, where you tell your prospective customers what they will get, what will happen

and why they should care.

5. **SAFETY** – The idea of safety is very comforting and is a core need.

6. **SAVE** – Even the wealthiest people shop for value. It's not just money that entices; people also want to know about saving time.

7. **YOU** – You're more likely to get your target audience involved if you address them directly.

8. **NOW** – This creates a sense of urgency for your future customer.

9. **EASY** – Most people want a quick and uncomplicated solution.

10. **COMPLIMENTARY** – Who can resist the granddaddy of them all?

Obviously, there are many other powerful words, and your list may vary depending on what you are selling. Try one or more of these words in your next advertising communication and see if it turns your lightning bug into lightning.

* Please note that most of these words should be avoided in your e-vertising campaigns. See "Key Words to Avoid in Your Next Email" in Section 6.

How to Elevate Your Ads from Good to Great

We've all seen them. Sometimes we're at home flipping through a magazine or trade journal. Maybe you're driving in your car listening to the radio. Or, you're sitting at home watching television. Suddenly it happens – that great ad that just grabs your attention and makes you want to buy.

So what makes a great ad great?

It Entertains – If you can't entertain or titillate your audience, then your ad is boring – plain and simple. And if your ad is boring, then you just wasted the cost of that media insertion because no one will engage. Remember, if you are asking someone to give you some of their valuable time, make it worth it.

Shock and Surprise – Predictability is boring. Great ads shock or surprise people in a way that gets them to remember your message and your product.

Get to the Point – There's no time to spare in ads today, so it's important that you get to the point – immediately. Make sure that your benefit is clear and easy to understand and your offer is obvious.

Keep Your Ideas Fresh – Just like fashion, ads can go out of style. Make sure that your ads are always consistent with current trends and styles. Be careful about recycling old ideas, unless you are sure that the market is ripe for them.

Coin a Catchphrase – One little phrase can make or break an ad campaign. Do you remember "Where's the Beef?" or "I can't believe I ate the whole thing" or "What happens in Vegas stays in Vegas"? If you can be this clever, imaginative or just plain lucky, your brand will live forever.

If You Try to Say Everything, You Say Nothing

We see it time and time again. Advertisers can't commit to emphasizing only those selling points that are most critical. Instead, they try to say everything. As a result, their main points get diluted and they end up saying nothing.

Whether it's a brochure, website, print ad or sales letter, there are some critical benefits or ideas in every marketing vehicle that are more important than others. Maybe you need to highlight a special price or a key benefit to your consumer. But your main messages are probably buried in your copy. We need to unbury them!

Ask yourself, "If someone looked at this and would only remember three things, what would I want them to remember?" No cheating – you have to pick no more than three, and be sure to rank them. Now that we know what they are, we have to give them proper prominence.

Avoid these typical mistakes.

- o Do not bold the key words. We've all seen the ads that have 30% of the copy bolded. It looks amateurish, and the bolding actually makes the copy harder to read.
- o Don't over-underline. The same idea applies to underlining. Underline a word or two and it's effective. Underline half the sentences and it becomes a blur.

Some strategies to consider.
So how do you effectively call attention to your most important messages? Try one or more of these tips:

- Cut the copy. Don't bury it in more words than necessary.
- Use a subhead to deliver a big punch.
- Use white space to create a "frame" around your important fact.
- Put a postscript (P.S.) on your marketing piece. Studies show a P.S. often has a much higher readership than your body copy.

Don't assume your audience will be able to sift out the information you consider critical. Make sure you don't make it even harder for them to find it. Instead, use some of these tips to take their hand and lead them right where they need to be.

Metaphorically Speaking

A recent study reported on research that demonstrated that when doctors explained to their patients how a new medicine would work by using a metaphor to describe the process, the drug actually worked better.

As marketers, we harness the power of metaphors as well. In fact, they're one of the most potent tools at our disposal. Take a fresh look at the products or services you sell. How can you equate them with words that draw a picture or conjure up an emotional response?

Some slogans or ad theme music haunt us because they have snuck past our intellect and grabbed hold of our imagination. Think of some taglines that just stick, such as one of our favorites from Timex: "Takes a lickin' and keeps on tickin'."

Contrast that with Pepsi's tagline, "It's the cola." Doesn't really register on the Richter scale, does it?

Read through your marketing pieces and look for opportunities to use a metaphor to bring your message to life. You'll be amazed at how people respond to emotionally charged words that paint a picture they can latch on to.

NOTES:

Get the Most Out of Your Creative Work

It's the most exciting part of any project – and usually the toughest – providing constructive feedback on a print ad, web design, logo concept, etc., that your creative team has presented. How do you judge whether it's on target or not? And if not, how do you move the process forward in a constructive and cost-effective way? Here are some tactics to think about.

1. Know Your Goals

Even if you share the same demographics and psychographics of your target customer, it's impossible for you to view your creative objectively, like a prospective customer would. You're too close to the inside process. Instead, research who your customer is and include that and all other specific targets for the ad in a creative brief. See that everyone involved in approvals agrees to the creative brief prior to developing the creative – to ensure a smoother process.

2. Strategy Is King

Compare what the ad is saying/doing to what you agreed it needed to do in the creative brief. Is it aimed at the right audience? Does it use language and visuals they will respond to? Does it clearly say why you're different from your competitors? The creative brief sets a target so that you can hit a bull's-eye with your creative.

3. It's Good to Be Bold

Does the creative feel safe? Then it's probably not going to grab attention. Resist the urge to play it safe or to be predictable. You'll never rise above your competition with "safe." With literally thousands of messages bombarding your prospects every day, you can't afford NOT to stand out.

4. Be Specific About Changes

It's okay to make changes. We expect you to! Just be specific about what needs to be different. Give direction. At the very least, point your team toward something or away from something. The worst thing you can tell your creative team is, "I don't like it, but I don't know why" or "I'll know what I'm looking for when I see it." Check against the brief and find where the creative work is not on strategy. Ask yourself if the change you want will impact the response rate, effectiveness or readability of the piece.

5. You Have the Power to Make Creative Great

Every piece of creative presented to you for review is like a baby to the team who created it. They've spent hours working on it, nurturing it, tweaking it. Even the simplest-looking design and copy has required many creative decisions before being presented to you. Colors are chosen to work best with a certain photo. A font is chosen to match the mood of the message. The headline is rewritten and dozens of options are tried out. The point here is not to discourage you from making changes, but to offer a suggestion about what changes to make. Working with your creative team, ask, "Did you try... " or "What was your thought process in choosing that font or that photo?" The more you know about the strategy that went into developing the creative, the more constructive your input will be.

6. Don't Catch the Dreaded "Change-a-Holism" Disease

You'll know you've got it when you find yourself making changes to the changes you've already made. This confusing and time-consuming situation mostly happens when new people are introduced into the review process at different times. To make the process efficient (and therefore as cost effective as possible for you), be sure everyone who has a say in approving the creative work – including legal – makes all their changes at the same time in the first round. When the process is running smoothly and professionally, you won't need more than two or three rounds before artwork is final.

Remember that great creative starts with you and how you work with your creative team. With these six steps, you'll be able to get creative work that is on target, that works better and that you really believe in!

NOTES:

Shaking Out Those Great Ideas

We've all had this happen to us. You need to come up with that great idea and your mind is drawing a blank. A recent study polled marketing professionals across the board and asked them how and where they got their best ideas.

As you may have guessed, the most frequent answer was in the shower (37%). Second on the list was in the car (24%). Third was while exercising (14%) and fourth was while eating or drinking (13%).

The most telling fact about this study was that only 12% of the respondents said their best ideas came to them while they were at work.

It would be easy to dismiss this as just a funny anecdote. But there is a serious reminder hidden within this study. As marketing professionals, we are expected to be creative and think strategically on command. We sit at our desks with distractions whirling around us. The phone ringing, email beeping, a co-worker's question or cute story about their weekend. And within all that chaos, we are expected to have our best thoughts.

So the next time you find yourself in a position of needing to find your best ideas and you can't seem to conjure them up at your desk – get out.

Try to shake yourself loose and change your surroundings. Drive around for a while. Take a walk in the park. Go to a toy store and play with the toys. Just let your mind wander and see where it ends up.

Can't sneak away? Then try working in someone else's office or in an unoccupied common space. This change in scenery can loosen up the thinking process for new ideas.

For some people, certain sounds or music allow them to free their mind. Maybe it's a tabletop water fountain, a certain CD or one of those background noise gizmos you get at The Sharper Image. The specifics aren't that important. What matters is that you find your own ways to jumpstart the process and shake the cobwebs and distractions so that you can tap into your best thinking on command.

And if all else fails, go home and hop into the shower!

How to Master the Small Space Ad

Many companies utilizing print media as part of the media mix, be it magazines, newspapers or newsletters, can't always afford to use full-page ads every time they advertise. Advertisers should consider small space ads as a tactic to extend the impact of their existing media budget.

Small space ads can be extremely effective. But all too often they are executed poorly, or they are not properly integrated into the overall media strategy. And guess what... they fail.

If you are going to use print advertising, and don't have the media budget of your larger competitors, you should utilize tactical small space advertising as a way to make your budget and marketing impact go further.

Here are some tips to help you reap the benefits from tactical small space advertising:

- o Remember that you only have two to three seconds to grab the reader's attention.

- o Don't try to fit two tons of potatoes in a one-ton truck. The most common mistake is to pack your small space ad with too many images or too much copy.

- o White space and simplicity are your best friends.

- o They have to be able to read it. Reducing the size of the type is only practical to a point. Try not to go smaller than 11-point type.

o   Use one strong single image that tells the story quickly.

o   When possible, use color for emphasis. Color will help grab attention and guide the flow of your ad for increased effectiveness. However, there are some exceptions to this rule. Ask your advertising agency for guidance on this if you're not sure.

o   Show your ad to a target sample. If they can't understand the ad in five seconds or less, start again.

Don't let a small advertising budget minimize your potential effectiveness. When done right, the small space ad can be a very powerful tactical tool that will help you generate more response for less. So think small and watch your profits grow.

Is Color Worth the Cost?

We've all wondered at some point or another if the extra cost to add color to a print ad or direct mailer would make a significant impact on the readership.

It may come as no surprise that the answer is yes. But you may not realize just how significant the impact of color can be.

A recent study found that changing your print ad or direct mailer from one-color to two-color will improve readership by over 17%. And changing that same one-color ad or mailer to four-color will improve readership a whopping 55%.

In addition to the significant increase in readership, the use of four-color in all promotional materials will enhance the overall image, credibility and sophistication of your company.

NOTES:

Are You Suffering from Insider's Blind Eye?

We all experience it. None of us are immune to it. We call it *Insider's Blind Eye*. IBE is an affliction that occurs over time as we get so immersed in the day-to-day operations of our companies that it becomes impossible to step back and take an objective look at ourselves from our customers' perspective.

There's nothing more eye opening than actually seeing your company through your customers' or prospects' eyes. And one of the best ways to make this happen is through a secret shopper.

Secret shoppers are the best of all worlds. They are impartial, and they experience your company just as an actual customer would. But they understand customer service, marketing and your company well enough to notice those little things that the average customer would feel but might not be able to articulate. A savvy secret shopper can help you identify areas where you lose sales, can improve retention or even add new services.

Don't try to take the shortcut on this. Your mom or next-door neighbor is not a good choice as a secret shopper. You want secret shoppers who can help you analyze your customers' experiences and enhance those experiences as they relate to your bottom line.

Don't think secret shoppers are only viable for retail businesses. We have successfully used secret shopping strategies for clients in various service, high-tech and manufacturing industries.

Like all well-crafted research initiatives, a well-defined secret shopping strategy can dramatically change the way you do business… for the better.

NOTES:

Why Should You Press Check?

In today's world of desktop printing and on-the-fly graphics, many marketers have forgotten the value of the press check. Why create great graphics if they are not produced to their fullest potential?

A good production manager is worth his/her weight in ink. They not only save you time and money, but they can make your printing dollars go much farther and increase the quality of the finished product as well. They understand color, inks, printing processes, vendor capabilities, paper selection, press sizes, printing techniques such as duo-tones, emboss and deboss, aqueous coatings and much, much more. These are all critical elements in creating the highest possible quality.

Here at Gumas, we are very fortunate to have a staff of highly experienced production professionals. Here are a few things that we look for when we do our press checks that you may want to incorporate if you do your own.

- o Check the color. Look for variations between your original expectations and the proofs. We pay particularly close attention to screened areas to make sure they are not lighter or darker than we want. Also, we always ask for densitometer readings of the color bars and check them for slurs.
- o Check the text layout. Look closely to see if the text wraps correctly from line to line. Look for any fonts that may have changed or shifted. In today's digital layout world, it's not uncommon for files to get changed from the original file to printer's proof and to the actual plate, especially if it has been sent electronically.

- Check to see if the photos are properly placed and cropped.
- On multiple-page projects, ask to see a paper "dummy" and the folded, backed-up proof. This will allow you to check the page sequence and final assembly. Check for creep and folding, especially crossovers. We always make sure to trim and fold our proofs just to make sure the layout is correct.
- For digital projects, be sure to request that your proof be printed on the actual stock whenever possible. Always get an ink draw down, especially if you are printing on a stock that is color or off-color. This gives you a real idea of what the final piece will look and feel like.
- Check the ink for consistency, especially where large solids are present, and ghosting and streaks on backup.

There are obviously many more signs to look for. We feel that these are the most basic and common and should be a critical part of any press check.

Image and brand is critical to your company's success. And a simple press check is a great way to make sure your printed materials project your company's best image.

Are Your Customers Laughing Behind Your Back?

Have you ever looked through a magazine and come across an ad that just looks bad? We all have. Now, have you ever wondered what your prospects and customers think when they come across one of your ads?

A recent study found that most print ads got very bad marks from readers. The study concluded that most ads, especially those in the B2B category, have become too much like "PowerPoint slide presentation" ads.

Below are some of the highlights of this recent study. As you read through this, take an objective look at your own advertising to see if you are guilty of any of these findings:

- o   74% of the respondents said that ads try to say or show too much, so the core message gets lost.
- o   66% felt the messages were too generic and did not address specific concerns or questions of the target audience.
- o   39% felt that ads were primarily company chest pounding.
- o   28% said that ads lacked passion or emotion.
- o   20% said the approach was too safe and did not take enough creative risks to get the audience's attention.
- o   19% believed ads contained expected stock photography or bad clip art.

So look at your own advertising closely. If your ads are guilty of any of the above, not only will your advertising be less effective or boring, more importantly, it may have a direct reflection on the perceived image of your company.

NOTES:

Are You Getting the Response You Want?

Have you ever wondered why some advertising programs generate an enormous response while others seem to fall flat? Your success may be dramatically enhanced with only a few adjustments. So what can you do to get your ads, direct mailers and other critical marketing materials to fall into the "enormous response" category more often?

Start with the basics.
Be sure to take the time to gain a thorough understanding of the basic playing field – including your target audience, your competition, the media in which the ad is running or the "list source" to which the mailer is targeted, as well as what it will take to get your target audience to buy from you. A good marketing partner should be able to provide this information.

Before you embark on your specific promotional program, understand what, if any, additional external issues you may encounter. Seasonal timing, pressure from the competition and other related factors can make each promotional piece unique unto itself. Be sure to adjust your program accordingly.

Grab their attention.
The first step in developing an effective promotional piece is to grab the attention of your target. An effective print ad or direct mailer must instantly communicate a simple-to-understand, benefit-laden message.

A powerful headline (of no more than seven to nine words) and a striking image will instantly draw your reader's focus. To make this exercise even more interesting, remember you only have about two to five seconds to accomplish this, because that's how fast the average person flips through a magazine or newspaper, or goes through each piece of mail.

Now pull them in.
So let's say that step one was a success and you've managed to break through the clutter and grab the reader's attention. The serious sales process with the prospect has now begun. At this point, the reader is intrigued enough by your message that they will give you another five to fifteen seconds of valuable time. Next, tell your story in such a way that the reader will be compelled to respond.

Talk benefits.
The body copy needs to tell your story quickly, outlining only those specific benefits that are the most important to the reader.

Make your story interesting and credible. It's okay to use subheads and bullet points. The best results occur when you develop highly creative messaging that provides your prospects with the competitive benefits they need to know about. Be sure to package the message carefully to brand your company in a memorable way.

Ask them to do something.
If readers have focused on your ad or direct mailer this long, then chances are they believe that you have something for them. Next, tell them what you want them to do. Ask them to call your toll-free number to receive a special offer, or to go to your website to get a free brochure. But be sure and tell them to do something that allows you to capture their names and bring the desired relationship to the next level. Again, be sure that your offer is credible and consistent with your ad message and strong enough to get a response.

And finally, measure your results and compare campaigns, to learn what your particular customer in your particular market needs to see to make a partnership with you. Focus groups and trial programs can be invaluable ways of honing in on what makes your market tick. Once you have a true understanding of this process and can design advertising to attract your target, you should see a measurable difference in your response.

NOTES:

Are You Giving Up Too Quickly on Your Advertising?

There you are, sitting at your desk trying to decide the best advertising strategy to use to promote your next project. You do your utmost to properly identify the target audience. You do your homework to analyze the competition. You painstakingly develop a strategic advertising plan that includes all of the tactical elements you feel will best reach the target. And finally, you develop a message strategy and creative look that you are confident will make prospective customers walk through the doors in droves.

So, with all this planning and enthusiasm (and money), you launch your advertising campaign that includes a good mix of interactive and print advertising, direct mail and radio. Then you sit back and wait for the results. After a couple of days, nothing happens. You wait another day or so, but only a trickle of activity. Now you start to get nervous. A week has now passed, and you're still not getting the results you were hoping to get. Now you start to panic and begin to pull the plug, and it all comes to a complete stop. It goes down in the books as a failed advertising campaign.

This entire process has not only cost you lots of money, but a lot of time and possibly a small dent in your marketing confidence. But maybe this advertising program that you worked so hard to develop and execute just wasn't out there long enough. What if you would have let it run its course just a bit longer? Would it have worked then?

How long should an advertising campaign be out there before you start to see results? How many direct mailers or emails does your prospect have to see before you can make the sale? How many print ads? How many radio or TV spots?

When it comes to generating awareness and sales, understanding the optimum level of frequency of exposure that each advertising campaign needs to have to be successful is just as important as the ad development itself.

A recent study sheds some very valuable light on this fact. This study confirms that most marketers give up too early and don't let their advertising campaigns run their course to success. The study revealed that, on average, 80% of sales leads are generated after a minimum of six to ten direct contacts with the prospect, yet less than 10% of advertising campaigns ever go beyond three contacts with the target customer.

This particular study followed the campaigns of numerous advertising programs across many industries and tracked their results over a set period of time. The typical advertising campaign within the study included either print, direct mail, email, outdoor or other signage, web and broadcast (radio or TV) vehicles or a combination thereof.

The findings of this study should be eye opening for any marketing professional that has ever lived through the scenario described at the beginning of this chapter. It confirms the value of frequency and consistency when it comes to breaking through the clutter and successfully convincing your prospect to buy.

When planning your next marketing campaign, be sure to remember that frequency is a very critical component to your success. As with any successful marketing program, your message must generate attention, pique interest and create a desire to do business with you. Once you have attracted the attention of your target audience, you need to stay on their radar screen until they are ready to buy. This may take more time than you thought, so be sure to accommodate this need in your initial marketing plan and budget.

Remember that no single ad, email, direct mail piece, billboard or radio spot can be expected to generate immediate results. When you develop your promotional campaigns, think of your advertising program as a growing garden. First you need to plant the seeds and continually tend to them. With your continued patience and nurturing, your garden will flourish, and you will soon harvest the fruits of your labor.

NOTES:

How Many Times Should an Ad Run Before It's Effective?

Years ago there was a very insightful study conducted that tested human recall when it comes to remembering advertising messages. The objective of this study was specifically focused on print advertising and how much the average reader recalled after reading the ad one time.

This study found that the average person recalls only about 20% of what they have read in a print ad. This same study also found that two-thirds of us forget the main benefit of what we have read after just one day. And after a week, almost 90% of us have completely forgotten everything we read in that same ad.

Now if you put this into perspective when it comes to your print advertising, it's estimated that each reader of a typical publication spends an average of just seven to ten seconds reading your ad. You can easily see that in order to be effective, you need to run your ads multiple times.

Repeating an ad ensures it will be seen and remembered.
Frequency is simply the number of times your ad runs. How many times is enough? Let's start by looking at some research that should help you better understand the dynamics of frequency, and how to use those dynamics to help you create a better advertising program.

One reason for repeating an ad is readership turnover. Another very critical reason why frequency is important is that we can't always predict when a buyer will be ready to buy. So whoever is lucky enough to be in front of their buyer at this critical point has the best chance of making the sale.

Repeating your ad significantly increases your recognition and message recall. Another recent study analyzed over 3,000 ads using a "remember seeing the ad" scale on each. Target consumers read various ads and then were asked to recall specific points in those ads. This study found that each ad's score increased in direct proportion to the increased frequency. The results showed that ads that ran less than three times during a 12-month period had an index of 81. Ads running 12–17 times during the same period increased the index to 112. And ads that ran 24 times or more in the same 12-month period scored a whopping index of 143.

This study shows that frequency does in fact increase return. But frequency also increases your budget. As an advertiser, you need to carefully consider how you allocate your budget to include the proper frequency to ensure success.

A Case History
We consistently see the power of frequency with advertising campaigns that we have created for our clients. A common mistake we see companies make is pulling their advertising before they've had a chance to penetrate the market and start generating results.

Recently, one of our clients who was working with a limited budget decided to run an advertising schedule in a well-known industry publication. The program featured a full-page ad that was scheduled to run in six consecutive issues of the publication.

After the second insertion, the client was discouraged with the results and was seriously considering pulling the plug on the campaign. After consulting with our client on the power of frequency, they decided to continue with the program. Good thing they did. After the third month, the ad started to generate a significant amount of qualified sales leads. Subsequent issues generated even more leads, which quickly turned into sales for our client. Not only was the original schedule kept, but also the decision was made to extend the program until leads started to slow down, which was about seven insertions later. That was our signal that our message was getting stale and it was time to for a change.

Frequency is just one element of a successful marketing program. When you incorporate the right frequency with the right media and the right creative message, and arrange each of these elements so they work together in perfect harmony, what you ultimately experience is the sweet music of success.

NOTES:

Smart Media Planning

It is very common for companies to actually overspend on print media placement to the point of diminishing returns.

When it comes to smart advertising, the creation and execution of a media plan is typically one of the marketing department's largest expenditures. The main goal is maximizing "reach and frequency." However, ultimate reach and frequency are usually very expensive, if not entirely cost prohibitive. Therefore, it is critically important that your media plan focus on those advertising vehicles that will reach the most prospects with the least amount of impact to your overall media budget.

Here's some food for thought: Research substantiates that, on average, purchasing the top two publications in a category delivers about 87% of the total readers in that category. Adding additional publications in that same category does not always mean greater results in proportion to the additional amount of money spent. In fact, the addition of a third publication in that same category typically only delivers an additional 5% to 6% reach. So remember: Spending more money doesn't always mean better results.

NOTES:

Specialized Versus Business Publications

Marketing in a business-to-business arena is full of endless media options. So how do you get the most return from your media strategy?

Successful advertisers have found that targeting specific messages to specialized niches makes their limited resources more effective. Specialized business publications deliver more targeted decision-makers than any other medium. This is where industry leaders spend their time and devote their interest. It's their first read of the day.

A recent study confirms that specialized business publications reach an overwhelming majority of business decision-makers versus general business magazines. The study also found that over 60% of these decision-makers subscribe *only* to specialized business publications and do not subscribe to any general interest magazines at all. In addition, 54% of these individuals are spending more time reading these publications than they did five years ago. And finally, the survey found that these decision-makers rate specialized publications as the most credible method for finding information about potential partners, vendors and suppliers.

So when you are deciding how to get the best bang for your media buck, look to specialized business publications first and tailor your creative message specifically to the audience of that publication. When executed properly, this strategy works.

NOTES:

Harness the Power of Trade Advertising

Simply put, trade advertising targets a specific niche. People who are serious about their industry read trade publications to get the latest information, to learn better ways to do things and to discover new products and services.

Unlike consumer or B2C (business-to-consumer) advertising, trade advertising brings with it a separate strategy for success. So what should you do to get the greatest return on your investment?

1. Remember who you're talking to.
Readers of trade publications tend to be more receptive to new information that can help their businesses. Since they are already thinking "business," advertising becomes less intrusive. In fact, when done properly, trade advertising becomes a helpful resource for the reader. This typically does not happen when you place an ad in a non-trade publication. Talk directly to the reader and say what your product can do for him or her. As with all advertising, keep your ad focused on a single, powerful message that grabs attention. Design your ad to reflect the look and style of your corporate brand.

2. Reach decision-makers.
A recent study confirms that trade publications reach an overwhelming majority of decision-makers. This study also found that over 60% of these decision-makers subscribe only to specialized trade publications and do not subscribe to any general interest publications. What may be the most telling result is that they rate trade publications as the most credible method for finding information about potential partners, vendors and suppliers. As a result, they are much more inclined to read the

ads in trade publications.

3. Does size matter?

Yes. In trade advertising, the size of an ad directly reflects the image readers will have of your company. In most cases, larger ads reflect a company that is solid, industry leading and will be around for years. This image comes across best in a full-page or spread ad. And, yes, a larger ad means more money. But it will be money wisely invested.

4. How often should you run your trade ad?

One of the great advantages of trade advertising is that recall is significantly higher when compared to consumer advertising. Typically, your non-trade ad will have to be read five to fifteen times before any action will be taken by the reader. In trade advertising, you could find success after just one insertion. However, we never recommend running only one ad, because good advertising is all about creating momentum and consistency.

5. Create a powerful ad.

So how should you go about maximizing your results? Here are some of the basics:

- o **Attract attention** – Focus on the most important benefit you offer prospects. And remember, this benefit must be based on what your prospects really want and not what you think they might want.

- o **Hold interest** – Once you've captured interest, hold it with information on what you are selling and why it's important. Use simple images to support your message and get it across faster. Short, simple sentences are best, as is copy that's believable and presented in everyday language.

o **Create desire** – Help prospects imagine what it would be like to own your product. Build desire by focusing on benefits, not features. A feature tells prospects what the product has. Benefits tell how that feature improves lives. And when it comes down to it, every prospect wants to know one thing ... what's in it for me?

o **Induce action** – Don't forget to say what you want prospects to do and when. An effective call-to-action must be clear and direct, relevant to customer needs and consistent with your brand. Most importantly, provide a sense of urgency or benefit for those who respond now.

Trade advertising is not for everyone. But if it falls within your strategic plan, and if you follow the thoughts outlined above, you should see results increase dramatically.

NOTES:

The ABCs of Measuring Media Effectiveness

Just about every successful marketing campaign has some type of media element. This could include print advertising (newspapers, magazines, etc.), interactive (digital media, SEO, email, etc.), broadcast (radio, television, etc.), out-of-home (billboards, bus boards, etc.), to name but a few options.

We find it surprising how many marketers do not completely understand the basic metrics of measuring media and how to best gauge effectiveness. So we thought it would be helpful to provide a cheat-sheet of common media measurement terms and definitions.

Reach – The number or percentage of different homes or persons exposed at least once to an advertising schedule in one or more media vehicles over a given period of time.

Frequency – The average number of times that the household or person is exposed to a media vehicle, schedule or campaign over a given time period.

GRPs – Also known as Gross Rating Points, they are the sum of ratings (reach x frequency) delivered by several media insertions in ten or more vehicles, where one point = 1% of the coverage base. For example, ten TV spots, each delivering an average rating of 15, deliver 150 GRPs, or 1.5 messages per average home.

Circulation – In print: the number of copies of a vehicle distributed based on an average number of issues. In out-of-home: the total number of people who are exposed to a vehicle within a specified time, typically a 24-hour period.

Share – The number of households or persons tuned to a particular program, expressed as a percentage of the total using the vehicle at a specific time.

Impression – Also referred to as exposure, it is a single view of an ad by a reader or TV viewer, a single hearing of a radio spot by a listener, etc.

This is only a general outline of the basic media measurements. There are many other ways to measure media effectiveness as it relates to your customized marketing program.

NOTES:

SECTION 4—GENERATING RESULTS

Now that you have identified your target audience and what you can offer them, how best to reach them? In our digital age, direct response advertising is still one of the most powerful ways to engage your customers and potential customers. Let's explore the best ways to get their attention and start a conversation that can blossom into a solid relationship.

How to Design Your Marketing Materials for Maximum Results

All marketing materials utilize some form of graphic design. Graphic design is a critical aspect of the overall perception and image of your company, and it plays a key role in the success of the specific promotional materials.

The design of your promotional materials has two primary objectives. First, it must generate attention in what is typically a very cluttered environment. Second, it must help the target audience quickly and easily absorb the information presented and why it will benefit them directly.

But what makes graphic design effective? Here are six very important features that all effective promotional material should incorporate to maximize response and overall penetration.

Have one dominant feature.

An effectively designed promotional piece has one dominant feature. This feature is typically an image or a headline. It is designed to catch the eye and draw the reader into the body copy or other sales messaging. Typically, you only have about two to four seconds to grab the attention of your targeted reader. A good rule to remember is to keep it simple – when you try to emphasize too much, you end up emphasizing nothing.

Minimize typeface variety.

Use one, maybe two, typefaces – total. Using too many typefaces upsets the flow and makes your piece harder to read. Remember that not only is the typeface contributing to a compelling story, it must effortlessly guide your reader to where you want them directed.

Text must be easy to read.

The text of any promotional piece is where most of the selling occurs. Type style is a very critical element that could dramatically increase the readability of your piece. Before you embark on writing your copy, have a good understanding of whom you are addressing, what style they would be most comfortable with and what would most likely get them to respond.

Type should not be too small or condensed. Narrow columns always read better than wider columns. Paragraphs should be short and to the point. Long-winded sentences and paragraphs typically scare readers away, especially those who have little time to devote to your sales message. Try using bullet points and subheads to break up text and help guide the reader through your message. The more inviting you make your copy, the greater the chance it will be read.

White space is good.

Don't be afraid of white space. You don't have to fill every inch of your promotional piece with copy and pictures. White space makes everything within it jump out and get noticed. Sometimes, saying less makes a bigger impact.

Use relevant images.

It's true what they say about a picture being worth a thousand words. Images in promotional pieces must help support your message, not confuse the target audience. One main image typically works better than multiple supporting images. Try to use an image that grabs the attention of the reader and draws them into your sales copy. But be careful not to use an attention-grabbing image that could portray the wrong image of your company.

Tell them what to do.

You've managed to get your target audience's attention. You've aroused their interest and desire. You've guided them through your clear and concise text. Don't leave them now. Most companies forget to include this very critical final step: Tell them to do something.

Make sure that all of your promotional pieces have a strong call-to-action built into the design. If a prospect reads to this point, you have someone who is very interested in what you have to say or sell. Tell them to buy. Tell them to call. Send them to your website to enter a contest. Just tell them to do something and watch them do it!

Creating effective promotional materials is not an easy process. It is both an art and a science. Many companies do not take these materials as seriously as they should, and, as a result, they never get the response rates or return-on-investment they are capable of achieving. So, whether you create your own materials or you have a professional firm create them for you, make sure you apply these simple, proven rules.

NOTES:

Seven Ways to Get Greater Results from Your Direct Response Program

More results. Better-qualified leads. Greater return on investment. Anyone who has ever developed direct response marketing, in any form, has undoubtedly heard one or more of these requests before. So what's a marketer to do?

In an effort to help you not only answer these requests but deliver upon them, we have put together what we feel are seven surefire strategies that you need to consider when creating your next direct response marketing program:

1. Always Remember the Basics – (a) Make sure your offer is made at the beginning. (b) Clearly tell targets what they will get and how they will benefit. (c) Tell them what action they must do. (d) Set a deadline. (e) Give as many ways as possible to respond.

2. Make Your Offer as Strong as Possible – Most direct response programs must have an offer to be successful. Common sense tells us the more compelling the offer, the better the results. Yes, offering a larger discount will get more response than a smaller discount. But before you start giving away too much of your margin, get creative. Find out what your target wants. For example, look into win-win partnerships with other companies, such as "Buy a driver from us and get a free putter from them," or "Order new doors from us and get a free hardware upgrade from them." Get the picture?

3. Why Won't People Buy? – Do your research to find out. Call them and ask them why they didn't respond. Get the specifics. Imagine what you could do armed with this information.

4. Tell the World Why Others Buy – Testimonials from satisfied customers can be powerful. Consider using real customers to tell their stories. Done right, they can be just the nudge it takes to get others to buy.

5. Test – Test lists, headlines, copy and offers.

6. Adjust Your Website – We are talking about more than just good optimization here. Make sure your website works closely with your direct response program. Or, better yet, consider a special landing page designed specifically for each direct response program.

7. Don't Forget Your Brand – Don't get caught up in the tactics of your offer. Remember to be true to your overall brand and what it stands for.

And just one final thought: It's not how much you spend, but how much you will earn that counts. As you put your budget together, consider the lifetime value of a customer versus the one-time cost of the direct response program. This may help you justify the investment it will take to be successful.

There are many more elements to successful direct response advertising, but if you include what we outlined above, you will be well on your way to greater results.

Five Ways to Turn Postcards Into Powerful Marketing Tools

Sometimes your advertising campaign could use a simple, inexpensive shot in the arm. The mailing of targeted and strategic direct mail postcards can be just what the marketing doctor ordered.

A postcard can easily attract the attention of your target audience. If designed right, postcards can break through the clutter and deliver to your target a very simple and impactful message. Here are our five rules of effective postcards that we have developed and used successfully for our clients.

Keep them simple.
Effective postcards must break through the clutter and grab your target's attention. The headline and main visual are your greatest potential attention-grabbers. Keep your message short, sweet and to the point. And be sure to deliver the benefit to your reader in five seconds or less.

Make them timely.
A real advantage of using postcards is that they are fast and easy to produce and distribute. Postcards are most effective when you have a message of timing, such as a product launch, grand opening, special offer or other similar time-sensitive promotion or announcement.

Use your real estate wisely.
We have found that oversized postcards with two sides work the best. On the main side, we suggest using the same tactics as when creating a print ad. You need to deliver a relevant and attention-grabbing message quickly. Use the other side (the

mailing side) to provide more details to support your claim and induce the action you want. Remember: Keep it brief. You don't want to cram your postcard with more copy than is needed.

Maintain your brand.

Your company brand is your lifeblood. Be sure to maintain its integrity in your creative messaging. Sure, it's "just a postcard." But the look and message you create is a direct reflection of your company and its brand.

Think big.

We always recommend oversized postcards (6" x 9" or larger) to break through the clutter and make your brand feel big. One of the advantages of postcards is that they don't come in an envelope. So not only does the large size grab attention, your creative message hits your target right in the face.

Postcards… We see them as simple, fast, inexpensive marketing powerhouses. Do them right and the results will put a smile on your face!

One Lump or Two?

We have talked a lot about how different types, sizes and shapes of envelopes can increase the effectiveness of a direct mail piece. We have also shared other tactics that could help you improve the results of your overall direct mail marketing campaigns.

But there's one direct mail technique in particular that we use that always seems to increase the response rates for our clients. We call it "lumpy mail." Lumpy mail is simply an envelope that contains something three-dimensional. This odd shape and feel makes opening the envelope hard to resist by the recipient.

For example, every few months, we all get that pen in the mail from a company who wants our business. Each time, we can tell it's another pen. We don't really need another pen. But we simply can't toss that envelope into the wastebasket. That's the power of the lumpy envelope.

You can get very creative with lumpy mail. Pick a theme, an item that always brands your company, a piece of hard candy, or how about a pen? Just about anything could work. And best of all, it's a very inexpensive way to get your standard envelope opened.

No matter which enticing lumpy mail option you choose, make sure whatever you send has some value and relevance to your message, your brand and your audience. Demonstrate that you aren't going to waste their time, even when jumping through hoops to get their attention.

NOTES:

Using Dimensional Direct Mail to Increase Sales

If you have ever tried to reach the C-level executive (CEO, CFO, CTO, COO, etc.) or another similar hard-to-reach target group, you know that a conventional mailing program rarely works. These individuals seem to have an army of people who act as gatekeepers to prevent unsolicited mail from ever hitting their desks.

It used to be that odd-sized mailers or hand-addressed envelopes could sneak past these gatekeepers. But nowadays, even these mailing attempts seem to get stopped at the door and ultimately meet their circular file death.

Effectively reaching the C-level executive.
So what's a marketing professional to do? The one tactic that we find to still work very well is the dimensional mailer, also known as the 3-D mailer.

Dimensional mailers can come in a box, a tube, a very puffy envelope or any other type of creative packaging that draws attention upon delivery. The package needs to be large enough and of sufficient quality so that the gatekeepers wouldn't dare throw it into the trash.

Developing a strategy that works.
So now you've managed to get your very creative dimensional package past the gatekeeper and into the hands of the ultimate decision-maker. Now what do you do? Effective dimensional mailers don't let the creativity stop there. Once the C-level executive opens your mailer, the real selling starts, so be sure to take advantage of this opportunity.

Remember, these people are very busy and may only give you a few seconds of their time to sell them your product or service, so make it count. Be sure that your mailer has some type of unique thingamajig inside, as well as very targeted promotional literature that tells your story quickly and credibly. Never send generic materials.

Here are two suggestions:

1. The first secret to a successful 3-D mailing is to make sure the object or gift that you include has some logical connection to your sales message. If it doesn't, it won't drive home your benefits and connect that gift to your product or company. Every day that your target executive looks at your cool thingamajig on their desk, they are reminded of your great products and services.

2. Get creative. Don't send golf balls or a coffee mug. That's too predictable. You need to stand out and get noticed. Send something that ties in to your message and will make your target think, chuckle and remember you.

An example.

We recently completed a 3-D mail campaign where the objective was to sell a product that would help accelerate the sales process for a targeted business group. The mailer we sent included a radar-baseball with the client's logo. When thrown, it would tell you how fast you pitched. We tied the product benefit together by emphasizing in our literature that with our product they could increase the speed in which they closed business and completely track their results.

When the sales team followed up, guess how many CEOs remembered the package and our message? You guessed it:

100%. The sales cycle still takes some time to close, but the mailing piece did its job and opened the door for the sales force.

NOTES:

The Power of a Cover Letter

In today's fast-paced world, sometimes we forget some of the old basics of marketing. We have found this to be true when it comes to direct response advertising.

Most direct mail marketing programs try to be very fancy by using elaborate and expensive mailers designed to present a sales message. These mailers usually work great. But we have found that sometimes, it's the old tried and true methods of direct marketing that can dramatically add results to your top-line revenue.

Take the lost art of the cover letter for example. Cover letters are proven persuaders when it comes to direct mail selling. They are personal, one-on-one sales messages that can dramatically improve the response rate of your direct mail program. That's why we recommend including a cover letter, even if it's just a short note. In fact, if the message can be conveyed in a brief note, that's even better.

What makes an effective cover letter?
Writing an effective cover letter is an art form in itself. An effective cover letter should have a headline followed by a one-sentence paragraph that states your case to the reader. The most read elements of a sales letter are the headline, the opening paragraph and the postscript (P.S.).

Some key elements when putting together a sales letter:
o   Write a headline that promises a specific benefit or result. The right cover letter headline has been shown to increase response by up to 20 times.
o   Grab the reader's interest with an engaging first

paragraph. Tell a short story or elaborate on the promise from the headline.

o Build value. People buy because what you're selling has more value than their money.

o Sell your uniqueness. Explain how and why your services offer more value than your competition.

o Summarize your benefits and give a price. The value you offer should seem virtually overwhelming when compared to the price.

o Give a guarantee.

o Compare risk to reward.

o Give credible and believable testimonials.

o Tell them how to order and provide them with as many order options as possible.

o Give a bonus for acting now.

o Use the P.S. to reinforce your main reason to act.

Consider adding a cover letter to your next direct mail program. The results may be astounding.

Direct Mail in Today's Security-Conscious Environment

If you are contemplating a direct mail campaign in the next few months, you need to be aware of a variety of challenges that could hamper even the best-conceived direct mail program.

The holiday season and its traditional increase in mail volume, combined with the threat of terrorist attacks, have created a new playing field for direct mail marketing.

Here is some advice to keep in mind before you undertake any direct mail program:

Consider peak mailing season.
Starting in November, mail volume piles up, with holiday cards and packages being sent by every household. So if you are mailing via bulk mail, be sure to add a *minimum* of ten days to your schedule. If timing is critical, first class postage is worth the extra cost.

Make sure your mail piece is properly identified.
The anthrax incidents have made us all a bit leery about opening our mail. You want people to open your mailing and not throw it away unopened. So make sure your mailings are boldly identified with your corporate image or a specific identifier that puts the recipient at ease.

Respect the intelligence of your prospect.
Many direct mail programs try to deceive the recipient into opening the mailer. Today's consumers don't appreciate deception. If you deliver a strong message and call-to-action, your prospect will respond.

Direct mail is one of the most efficient ways to target an audience. If you have truly identified the appropriate individual within the prospective organizations, direct mail is a perfect medium to convey your message. So tell your prospects what you expect them to do (strong call-to-action), give them enough mechanisms to respond (BRC, URL and phone number), provide a compelling reason to purchase your product and keep in mind the current postal environment. Then watch your sales team capitalize on a successful direct mail campaign.

Getting the Most from Your Signage and Billboards

Just about every company invests in some form of outdoor advertising – this includes billboards, banners, building signage, on- and off-site signage, bootlegs and other similar signage designed to get a message out.

We have found that most outdoor advertising does not produce the expected results. It's not that the signage was poorly designed or produced. In fact, most of what we see is very expensive to produce. The problem lies in understanding the dos and don'ts of outdoor advertising and what this potentially powerful medium should deliver.

Effective signage.
Let's take a closer look at some of the creative and graphic design elements that are essential to effective billboard and signage development.

The design of your outdoor has two primary objectives. First, it must generate attention. Second, it must help the target audience quickly and easily absorb the information presented. The average outdoor advertising unit has about three to four seconds to attract the eye of the target and get them to absorb your message. So billboards need to be treated differently than conventional collateral materials.

But what makes outdoor graphic design effective? Here are the components we consider most critical when producing billboards and signage.

Have one dominant feature.

An effectively designed unit has one dominant feature, typically an image or a headline that catches your eye and draws you in. Keep it simple – when you try to emphasize too much, you end up emphasizing nothing. A good rule to remember is to keep the verbiage to no more than seven words. This allows your message to be read quickly, and your benefit is remembered.

Minimize typeface variety.

As with other printed marketing materials, use one, maybe two, typefaces – total. Typestyle is very important to the overall readability and effectiveness of your outdoor. For example, you can use typeface in bold for the headline and non-bold for other text to create visual appeal without it becoming too busy or hard to read.

White space is good.

Don't be afraid of white space. You don't have to fill every inch with copy and pictures. Sometimes saying less makes a bigger impact than saying more.

Keep your concept simple.

All signs must be simple to understand and easy to read. This may be one of the most critical aspects of your strategy, so don't take this area lightly. Don't use typefaces that are "too fancy" or may cause confusion. Don't use visuals that are hard to see or understand quickly. Remember that you don't have long for your message to be absorbed.

Use relevant images.

Images in outdoor and signage must help support your message, not confuse the target audience.

One main image typically works better than multiple supporting images. Remember that your target audience is usually on the move when they see your outdoor advertising. So make your image relevant and obvious so you can drive home your sales message quickly.

Make it readable.

We have found that a largely overlooked problem lies in the sign's inability to be read at a distance. Before you begin the design of any outdoor advertising, make sure you know where it will be posted and what the approximate viewing distance will be.

To help you maximize your signage and its viewing effectiveness, try using this handy viewing distance chart that we've developed to help our clients get the most from their signage. Optimum audience viewing distance is listed below, followed by the minimum recommended letter height for maximum readability.

100 feet = 4 inches
250 feet = 10 inches
360 feet = 16 inches
500 feet = 22 inches
1,000 feet = 43 inches
1,320 feet = 57 inches

Remember that these numbers represent the minimum recommended height. Factors that may require you to bump up the size include color scheme, font selection and sign placement.

Outdoor advertising can be a very powerful tool when used properly. Don't let your out-of-home promotional message get lost simply because you didn't know these proven dos and don'ts. Follow these layout tips and size recommendations, and your signage will deliver maximum results.

NOTES:

SECTION 5—WEBSITE STRATEGY

Your website is an essential part of your company's marketing plan. An engaging, user-friendly website that complements your other marketing efforts will do wonders for your credibility and strengthen your brand. We're going to give you the tools to create an effective online presence that will get you noticed.

The Internet Continues to Impact Business

A recently commissioned study of Internet use by C-level and other senior-level corporate executives (senior VP and above) shows the substantial impact the web is having on the way in which business will apparently be conducted in the future.

C-level Internet Usage

Without a doubt, the Internet is already a huge part of the senior-level executive's workday, and what's even more telling is that those senior executives are actually clicking on ads. The study found that mornings present the best time to reach the lion's share of senior executives. For example, over half the C-level respondents admitted that they access the web before they go to work. By contrast, only 41% of the respondents said they read a newspaper before going to work.

This study concludes: "These results reflect a now irrefutable truth – that the web has become an integral part of a senior executive's business day." "That C-level managers are logging onto the web in the morning before reading a newspaper is proof that the web truly is the medium of choice for senior-level business decision-makers."

Online research is becoming very common among C-level respondents, with 58% using the web for this purpose, while only 33% use the web to check their stock portfolios. Only 11% delegate online research to their assistants.

C-level Email

Of little surprise is that 82% of C-level executive respondents said they check their email before they start other work. And only 6% said they have an assistant do it for them. However, what is surprising is that 48% of C-level respondents say they click on online ads when they "see something of interest."

So if the senior-level executive is part of your marketing target customer, be sure that you have a strong online component.

Harness the Power of Online Marketing

Let's take a look at one of the most successful marketing tools available: the online campaign.

Integrate online and conventional marketing.
Adding an online aspect to a conventional marketing strategy can significantly enhance your return on investment, as online campaigns are among the greatest response-boosters available.

Even the most simplistic online presence gives customers and prospects immediate gratification by being able to access information 24/7. And it puts them in charge of how much and when they want to drill down for additional material.

Drive traffic to your site with an offer.
Because online media can capture information inexpensively, it is a great way to build a one-on-one relationship with your prospects and customers.

Offer people a reason to come to your site. For example, if you are a builder promoting a new home community with an Italian theme, offer an "enter to win" promotion where prospects who sign up at the website enter to win a free dinner at a local Italian restaurant, an Italian cooking class or something else along these lines. You can really get creative here. Once the prospect is at your site, you can capture key data. Most people are willing to give up a limited amount of information in order to qualify for something they deem valuable. You'll be establishing a relationship with your prospects while also building a database for the future.

Full disclosure is important. Be sure to post a privacy policy that lets visitors know how their information will be used. Even if you don't plan to share information with others, let visitors know how you plan to communicate with them in the future.

Customize each campaign with a micro-site.
When a prospect sees an ad, a brochure or any marketing piece that carries your theme, be sure that theme is also present at your website.

Instead of overhauling your site with every new campaign, we recommend that our clients do this the quick and easy way – by adding a micro-site.

A micro-site is a mini website that typically has a short lifespan (several weeks to several months) and a limited number of pages. It acts as an interim landing pad that connects the current campaign and the corporate website.

We recently helped a builder create a series of micro-sites to carry the specific design, theme and messaging of their numerous projects. The sites provided a seamless transition for the prospect and enabled the company to quickly coordinate their offline and online creative styles without making major, and costly, changes to their primary corporate website – a "win-win" for all.

Because micro-sites allow precise tracking of traffic, they are also the wave of the future for measuring response rates.

Personalized password-only entry boosts response.
The more you can personalize your marketing activity, the better your response. So a personalized web experience can dramatically improve the effectiveness of marketing efforts. For

example, offer a personalized password or code on each direct mail piece, brochure or coupon. Ask the prospect to enter the information online to enter a contest, complete a survey or qualify for other premium offers. Most people can't resist checking to see what their very own personal code will get them, and you have another way of developing that important relationship.

Because of the speed of change of online tools, be sure to re-evaluate your online marketing campaigns at least every six months, if not sooner. We recommend a thorough audit by an outside agency on a regular basis. Such careful consideration of how you reach your valued customers is bound to pay off many times over.

NOTES:

Is Your Website Keeping Up?
(Part 1 of 2)

First impressions are critical. Most businesses go to great lengths to make sure their sales centers are perfect. Unfortunately, most do not go through the same exercise with their websites. Like the sales center, your website dramatically affects the overall impression of your organization.

Take a few moments to assess your site's strengths and weaknesses. Start by trying to view it from a prospective customer's point of view. Would you choose to do business with this company? Does your homepage say everything you want about your organization? Does it differentiate you from your competition? Is it easy to navigate?

Design for the user.
As the Internet matures, so do visitor sophistication and expectations. Visitors want site navigation to be clear, simple and consistent from page to page. They want to be able to find information fast.

What does this mean for your web strategy? First of all, don't design and write your website as you would your other marketing collateral pieces. An effective site must focus on how quickly you can communicate what you need to say in a way that is relevant to the targeted reader. You must understand their time restraints and level of sophistication. Unlike outbound advertising, web visitors come to you, so your site should be less hype and more informational. Place your most important information near the top to limit scrolling and keep visitors focused.

Ideally, your site should be an easy-to-use reference. It needs to instill credibility, and must ultimately lead to acquiring a new customer or retaining an existing one. It should invite your customers to revisit every time they have questions, thus saving them time and money.

What do your customers want?

Your website is a critical source of information for potential buyers. In our tech-savvy environment, these customers go to the web first, so make sure to give them the information they want, create the image they expect and understand their every need.

Make sure the site is easy to navigate and enjoyable to visit. If it becomes a chore for users to find what they are looking for then the odds of keeping those visitors diminishes greatly.

Get them involved.

Customers want to find out everything they can about the product and options you have to sell. The key is to not only present the information they want quickly and easily but to also find a way to keep visitors coming back to your site. Update your site regularly – with new information and images. The more you update, the more reason prospects have to come back and stick around.

Look at every page independently.

On a practical level, remember that Internet users don't always enter your website from your homepage. Check to make sure that each page can stand on its own. This may mean reiterating key selling benefits in a variety of ways, while maintaining clarity and avoiding ambiguity throughout each page of your site.

Because of its power to bring in new customers, your website requires extensive and ongoing focus from you and your marketing partners. In Part 2, we'll look at specific ways to power up your design and get the most out of this important tool.

NOTES:

Is Your Website Keeping Up?
(Part 2 of 2)

How well is your website working for you? With technology changing by leaps and bounds, it's critical that this most important marketing tool is up to date in every way. This is the second in a two-part series on how to quickly assess whether your website needs updating, and where best to put your marketing dollars.

Don't forget the basics.
In the rush to update their websites with new technology and the buzz that goes with it, some companies are unfortunately losing ground by moving away from basic, tried-and-true marketing concepts. Your website is a critical marketing tool, but don't ramp it up so quickly that you leave customers, and common sense, behind. These simple tips offer a quick review of whether your site is up to speed:

o **Keep it simple** – Simplicity is the golden rule for all forms of marketing, especially websites. Make sure your site is easy to understand and to navigate. If visitors must search your whole site for basic information, chances are they will leave before finding what they need. Keep the fancy graphics and effects to a minimum.

o **Less is more** – An effective website provides only the information your reader needs. Be concise. A good rule of thumb is to cut the number of words you use in your printed collateral in half. If you feel more information is needed, provide links to other web pages, separate from your main pages, which your visitor can click on to get those additional details.

- o **Think visually** – Providing information in "visual bursts" will guide your reader to your information quickly and easily. Economize the number of words to allow visitors to move quickly through each page's offerings. Try the following:
  - Use headlines and subheads to guide the reader.
  - Use bullet points to emphasize key benefits.
  - Choose shorter words over longer ones.
  - Limit paragraph length to three sentences. The web may be the only marketing vehicle where one-sentence paragraphs are not only allowed but also preferred.
  - Place important concepts at the beginning of sentences.
  - Place important sentences at the beginning of paragraphs.
  - Write in the active voice ("Bob purchased the home," and not, "The home was purchased by Bob.")

- o **Consistency. Consistency. Consistency.** – All elements of your website should tie together like a well-told story. The consistent look and feel should extend to your entire communications strategy to support and enhance your overall brand.

- o **Know your visitors** – Get inside your customers' heads and find the main hook that will connect them to your products and services. Do some research; go to tradeshows; hang out in your information center; respond to customer service emails; talk directly to customers and prospects. Effort spent knowing whom you're trying to reach will pay off many times over.

o **Try this simple test** – Ask several people outside of your company to visit your website. Give them ten seconds to review your homepage. If, after ten seconds, they can provide a description of your company and its products and services that meets your brand image, then chances are you have an effective site. If not, then you have some work to do!

Your website is an extension of your marketing campaign. It reflects your brand and your culture. But most importantly, it is a main portal through which all outside visitors can learn about your company and your brand. You have just one chance to welcome these visitors. Make sure that you take full advantage of this opportunity.

NOTES:

Website Design

In today's e-commerce/e-business age, having an effective website is critical to the success of any business. When developing a website, you must understand those strategies that will make your site most useful for your customers and prospects.

Among the thousands of B2C sites on the web, it seems that all too many of them are not designed for the specific needs of the customer. Cluttered with graphics, Flash and other animation, these sites are not user-friendly and take too long to deliver their messages. Rather than trying to provide visitors with easy answers to the questions they came for, many visitors leave with even more questions.

Here are four tips to keep in mind when creating a powerful website:

1.   Keep it simple. Make sure your site is easy to understand and navigate. If you force the visitors to search your whole site for basic information, chances are they will leave before finding what they need. Keep the fancy graphics and effects to a minimum.

2.   Answer the basic questions. Give your visitor the basic information they need about your company, such as who you are, what you do, where you do it, how to obtain your services and most important, what you can do for them. And always include your phone number.

3.   Design it for your target audience. When designing the site, remember who you are designing it for and cater to

their needs and expectations, not yours.

4.   Create an extension of your customer services. Ideally, your site should be an easy-to-use reference that instills credibility and ultimately leads to acquiring a new customer or retaining an existing one. It should invite your customers to revisit every time they have questions, thus saving them time and money.

Effective Website Eye Flow

So you want to create the most effective website possible? Where should you put your most critical data? How should the homepage be designed to maximize readability?

A recent study used advanced eye-tracking data to finally answer many of these pressing issues. Eye tracking is a process of mapping a user's eye movement across a computer screen and assessing the amount of mental strain exerted at any given moment.

This study focused primarily on homepage viewing. Here are some of the findings with the most impact:

1. Homepages are generally viewed as portals to help visitors get where they want to go. They should not be lengthy destination pages, but should provide visitors with a quick overview and links for additional information.

2. Web visitors look to the upper-middle section of the homepage first. Positioning your navigation tools there allows visitors to get where they want to go fast. Almost 20% of visitors' attention focuses on this spot.

3. Text-heavy homepages are more difficult to use. Most visitors only read the first two lines before moving on.

4. Clean, uncluttered sites produce higher success rates. Visitors don't want to filter through unnecessary information.

5. Buttons or icons with one- to three-word descriptions get the most use. Wordy buttons/labels are used least.

6. On average, banner ads receive about 13% of the visitors' time and interest.

Remember: Before you design your website, make sure that you treat it just like any other visual medium. Pay close attention to your homepage. Establish a flow pattern for your visitors' eyes to follow. The easier you make it for your visitors, the better they will understand and receive your message.

How Well Is Your Website Optimized?

Let's say you and your family want to go on a cruise to the Caribbean. If you're like most people, you'll head straight for Google, Yahoo or one of the other major search engines and type in what you are looking for. The results that come back do not happen by accident. Those results are part of a powerful marketing strategy called search engine optimization, or SEO.

So, how do you get your company to come up when your customers search the Internet? The detailed answer to that question is much too long and complex for this forum, so we have outlined some basic "on-page" factors that you can implement immediately. These are adjustments to the format and text on your website that should help your site increase its rankings. Here are just a few suggestions:

o Determine how your customers and prospects search for you or your competitors and make a list of the most commonly used search words or phrases.

o Once you determine these keywords and phrases, make them an integral part of your web message.

o Make sure that those keywords and phrases are strategically placed throughout your website — and make sure they are grammatically correct.

o Be realistic with the phrases you choose. If they are too generic, you will get lost in the crowd.

For instance, let's take our example of a cruise. If a cruise operator selected its key phrase to be "cruise," chances are it would not be successful since "cruise" is so generic and is used by so many. They would increase their chances by changing the key phrase to "Caribbean cruise." And they would increase their chances even further if they used "five-day Caribbean cruise."

For a real-world example, try this test: Come up with two to three search phrases (one to three words long) that you'd like your site to come up high on the search results for. Type these into Google, Yahoo or any one of the other major search engines. If your company comes up, then congratulations, you've passed the test. If it doesn't, then you need to seriously consider a comprehensive SEO plan.

Improving your SEO has green benefits as well. Web marketing is generally greener than using paper and materials to promote your goods and services. So improving your website's performance via SEO allows more people to learn about you without increasing the amount of resources needed — and that is good business all around.

Want to Increase Your Website Traffic?

If you were to ask most marketing professionals how to increase the traffic to your website, the recommendation would likely be to spend more money on advertising to drive visitors there. Sure, that's one way. But before you go to all that expense, try this method first.

In most cases, you can increase your website's traffic by simply rethinking your page headers and meta tags.

The average web surfer finds what they're looking for via the many search engines that exist. They may or may not know of your company. But they are looking to solve a particular problem, in search of a needed product or service, or just want an answer to a question.

Most search engines work by taking a combination of words that the surfer inputs into their search criteria and then locates the web pages that contain those exact words.

Here's a recommendation. Go through your website page by page. Look at its content and imagine you are a prospect of your company. What would you type into the search box? Now, make sure that those key words appear in key locations on your website and in the meta tags.

As a test, check your traffic logs just before you make the changes to your site. After about 30 to 60 days, check those traffic numbers again to see how much they've increased. You should be happily surprised.

NOTES:

How to Place Your Website Higher in Search Engine Results

When a prospect is searching the Internet for a company in your industry, how does your website stack up against your competition?

There are many factors that affect the results of Internet search engines, but one area that many of our clients overlook is their title and keyword selection.

What's in a title?
The title is that strip of language that's in the very top border of your browser. It should identify what's on that page. Every page on your site should have a title tag that starts with the key phrases and words that most accurately describe the content of that particular page. Title tags may show up in search results, so try not to use the same title tag throughout your website.

Choosing the right keywords.
Like any good marketing strategy, your keywords must be carefully chosen and relevant. Be sure to choose words that your customers and prospects might use if they were using a search engine to find you.

Be specific and use targeted keywords. You have a better chance of being found if your keywords come up as one of twenty-five results, versus coming up as one in one thousand results. For example, if you are a bed and breakfast in the wine country of California, you may wish to reconsider using "B & B" as one of your generic keywords. How many B & Bs do you think are on the web? Chances are you will be listed among thousands. Perhaps a more targeted choice might be "Sonoma B & B."

Get creative, and try not to optimize your homepage for every one of your site's keywords. Instead, focus on three or four keywords that are relevant per page. Spread out the related words onto other pages within your site. This will create additional entry points for visitors to enter your site when they use search engines. Since each page is targeted at specific phases, each will score higher than a "one-size-fits-all" solution.

Get specific.

It's very tempting to try to cast your net as far and as wide as possible with keywords. But you will find far better results if you zero in with a more targeted approach. This strategy lets you focus on what really differentiates you from your competitors. This strategy also results in higher placement for your site in the search engine results.

Internet Usage Patterns Can Enhance Your Results

A recent study has helped us to understand online usage patterns much better. For the first time, this study provides clear evidence that five distinct dayparts do exist on the Internet. Each of these dayparts displays significant differences in usage levels, demographics and type of content accessed.

Savvy marketers can use this information to improve the efficiency of their online marketing activity and interactive media buys by weighting their efforts toward those dayparts in which their target audiences are available in the greatest numbers.

A daypart is classified as a consecutive block of time on similar days (weekdays or weekends) during which the size of the audience is homogeneous, as is the characterization of the group using the medium. They are:

Early morning (M–F, 6 am–8 am)
Daytime (M–F, 8 am–5 pm)
Evening (M–F, 5 pm–11 pm)
Late night (M–F, 11 pm–6 am)
Weekends (Sat–Sun, all day)

Some key findings of this study included:

o   Daytime is the largest daypart (measured in both total audience and total usage minutes) followed by evenings and weekends.
o   Affluent, working people between the ages of 25 and 54 make up the largest share of the daytime audience than any other daypart.

- Children under age 18 are three times more likely to be reached during the evening or weekend dayparts.
- Internet utilities, such as search engines, email and chat rooms show very little variation in usage by daypart. Online content sites, in contrast, show distinct differences in usage by the time of day.
- Use of news and information sites is concentrated in the early morning and daytime dayparts.
- Entertainment and sports sites usage increases dramatically during the evening and weekend dayparts.
- On average, e-commerce activity is growing and now accounts for 5.3% of time spent online. A considerably larger share of e-commerce occurs on evenings and weekends than during the daytime.

As you can see, using the Internet to supplement your existing marketing is a wise use of your marketing dollars. The more you can direct those dollars to where and when your target audience is actually online, the greater your return on investment.

NOTES:

SECTION 6—ONLINE MARKETING

The world is spending more and more time online, and email marketing provides one of the fastest-growing methods of reaching your target audience, from teens to seniors. This section will tell you all you need to know to make sure you're taking advantage of this flexible, cost-effective vehicle.

Email Marketing 101

Most savvy business people have a good understanding of marketing tactics. They know they must develop a good branding strategy for their communities and company. They know they also need to create powerful ads, signage, direct mail and web presence to generate traffic and sell more.

But the one strategy many still don't fully use is email. When properly used, email marketing can provide a significant boost to marketing results.

Email marketing has many advantages – no printing or postage costs, and total control over when and how the message is delivered.

Here are some tips for your campaign:

1. Creative preparation is a must.
Email marketing can be one of the most effective or ineffective marketing tools around. Where you land depends on your creative preparation. Review these messaging questions as you begin:
  o Can you quickly translate the product's features into benefits that matter?
  o What specific action do you want from the recipient? To ask for more information? Visit a model home? Join the interest list? Buy?
  o How will responses come in? Email? Website? Telephone?
  o What branding standards do you need to incorporate? Will they properly translate via email?
  o What are the legal mandatories? Terms and limitations?

2. Carefully create your subject line.

Just like the outside envelope of a conventional mailer, the subject line is the most critical part of an email. It's what grabs attention and gets someone to look inside. Carefully craft this line, using a copywriter's touch. Make it short and to the point, with an ideal length of four to six words. Identify your company so recipients know the email is from a credible source. (See "Email Marketing – Crafting Your Subject Line" later in this section.)

3. Give them something they can use.

Because email inboxes are in general 60% fuller than they were last year, people are selective about what they open. A sales pitch alone may not be enough. In addition, offer something of value. Present an incentive to purchase or helpful information that brings the community and your company to life.

4. Keep it simple.

Most systems can read HTML emails, so a strategically targeted, HTML graphic email campaign will get your point across, and provide branding support, almost every time. Although tempting, avoid rich media, such as Flash or streaming video, as many people still live in a low-tech world and are not capable of reading these types of graphics.

5. Maximize your content.

Because long-winded emails are quickly overlooked, make your message clear and to the point. Write for your reader's benefit and knowledge level, not your own. Bring your company to life by adding visuals when possible. Provide a forum for responses and questions, and then answer those communications quickly.

6. Use color properly.

In the web world, color is not all that meets the eye. A font color tag not formatted within the web-safe color palette may be difficult for your recipient to read. Avoid background colors other than white. If you do use a background color, remember that black is the safest, while green, cyan, magenta and yellow are the riskiest.

7. Include a signature line.

A signature line significantly reduces the chances of your email getting caught in anti-spam software. It also adds credibility and personalizes your message. Just be sure to keep the signature short and sweet.

8. Test before launching.

When the email is polished and ready to go, take one more step to ensure success. Conduct a small test, just as you would in a conventional direct mail program. Try a few options on select customers or a focus group, and choose the plan that proves most effective.

Your email program can significantly assist your marketing efforts. Use it to stay in front of prospects in a cost-effective way. Use it to position yourself as an industry expert. Use it to find referrals. However you choose to use it, we suggest that you add it to your marketing mix as soon as you can.

NOTES:

Email Marketing Terms You Should Know (Part 1 of 2)

In Part 1, we will highlight the marketing-specific email terms you need to know. In the next part, we will focus on the technical terms. We hope this helps you to better understand the world of email marketing.

(1) Email newsletter ads or sponsorships – Buying ad space in an email newsletter or sponsoring a specific article or series of articles. Advertisers pay to have their ad (text, HTML or both, depending on the publication) inserted into the body of the email.

Email newsletter ads and sponsorships allow advertisers to reach a targeted audience and drive traffic to a website, store or office, entice sign-ups to a newsletter or promote sales of a product or service.

(2) Permission-based email – Email sent to recipients who have opted in or subscribed to receive email communications from a particular company, website or individual. Permission is an absolute prerequisite for legitimate and profitable email marketing. Every company should have a permission-based program.

(3) Viral marketing – A type of marketing that is carried out voluntarily by a company's customers. It is often referred to as word-of-mouth advertising. Email has made this type of marketing very prevalent. Tools such as "send this page, article or website to a friend" encourage people to refer or recommend your company product, service or a specific offer to others.

In addition, there are strategies where you can induce and support your own online viral campaigns. (See also "Word-of-Mouth Marketing 101" and the three-part "ABCs of Viral Marketing" later in this section.)

(4) Targeting – Selecting a target audience or group of individuals likely to be interested in a certain product or service. Targeting is very important for an email marketer because targeted and relevant email campaigns yield a higher response and result in fewer unsubscribes. Make sure your conventional and email targets are compatible.

(5) House list (retention list) – A permission-based list that you've built yourself. Use it to market, cross-sell and up-sell, and to establish a relationship with customers over time.

Your house list is one of your more valuable assets because it is seven times less expensive to market to an existing customer than it is to acquire a new one. Use every opportunity to add to it and use it.

(6) Rental list (or acquisition list) – A list of prospects or a targeted group of recipients who have opted in to receive more information about certain subjects.

Using permission-based rental lists, marketers can send email messages to audiences targeted by interest category, profession, demographic information and more. Renting a list can cost between 10 cents and 80 cents per name. Be sure your rental list is a certified, permission-based opt-in list. Permission-based lists are rented, not sold. Don't be fooled by a list offer that sounds too good to be true. Save the $19.95 and buy yourself a George Foreman Grill instead. Unlike the cheap list, the grill is worth the money.

(7) CPM (cost-per-thousand) – In email marketing, CPM commonly refers to the cost per thousand names on a given rental list. For example, a rental list priced at $250 CPM would mean that the list owner charges 25 cents per email address.

(8) Open rate – The percentage of emails opened in any given email marketing campaign, or the percentage opened of the total number of emails sent.

(9) Email blocking – Email blocking typically refers to blocking by ISPs. Emails that are blocked are not processed through the ISP and are essentially prevented from reaching their addressed destination. ISPs actively block email coming from suspected spammers.

NOTES:

Email Marketing Terms You Should Know (Part 2 of 2)

We outlined some important marketing-side email terms in Part 1. This part will focus on the technical side. We hope you find this helpful.

(1) Above-the-fold – A term carried over from the newspaper business literally meaning above the fold or crease in the paper. It is the part of a web page that is visible without scrolling. It is generally the more desirable placement on a website because of its visibility.

If you have a "join our mailing list" tag on your website, you should place it "above-the-fold," making it easy for visitors to opt in.

(2) Opt in (or subscribe) – To opt in or subscribe to an email list is to choose to receive email communications by supplying your email address to a particular company, website or individual, thereby giving them permission to email you.

The subscriber can often indicate areas of personal interest (e.g., golfing) and/or indicate what types of emails she wishes to receive from the sender (e.g., newsletters, new product info, etc.).

(3) Opt out (or unsubscribe) – To opt out or unsubscribe from an email list is to choose not to receive communications from the sender by requesting removal of your email address from their list.

(4) CTR (click-through rate) – Expressed as a percentage, it is the number of unique clicks divided by the number that were actually opened by recipients that click on a given URL in your email.

(5) Conversion rate – The number or percentage of recipients who respond to your call-to-action in a given email marketing campaign or promotion. This is the measure of your email campaign's success. You may also measure conversion in phone calls, appointments, sales, etc.

(6) HTML email – An email that is formatted using Hypertext Markup Language instead of plain text. HTML makes it possible to include unique fonts, graphics and background colors. HTML makes an email more interesting and, when used properly, can generate higher response rates than plain text.

(7) Hard bounce/soft bounce – A hard bounce is the failed delivery of an email due to a permanent reason like a nonexistent address. A soft bounce is the failed delivery of an email due to a temporary issue, like a full mailbox or an unavailable server.

(8) Signature file (or sig file for short) – A tagline or short block of text at the end of an email message that defines the sender and provides additional information such as company name and contact information. Your signature file is a marketing opportunity. Use it to convey a benefit, and include a call-to-action with a link.

(9) Spam or UCE (unsolicited commercial email) – Email sent to someone who has not opted in or given permission to the sender. Do you get spam? (A rhetorical question, to be sure.) Find out how the sender obtained your email address.

(10) Privacy policy – A clear description of a website or company's policy on the use of information collected from and about website visitors and what they do, and not do, with the data.

Your privacy policy builds trust, especially among those who opt in to receive email from you or those who register on your site. If subscribers, prospects and customers know their information is safe with you, they will likely share more information with you, making your relationship that much more valuable.

NOTES:

The ABCs of Outbound Email Marketing

We've all been victims of spam – it's very annoying. The good news is that there are increasingly effective laws designed to slow some of that unsolicited email that clogs our inboxes every morning.

But even with the proliferation of spam, outbound email is still an extremely effective marketing tool. Don't shy away from using it if it makes sense. You just need to know how to use it wisely.

To comply with the law, all of your email marketing messages should include the following:

Your name in the "From" field.
Studies show people look first to the "From" or "Sender" to decide whether or not to delete the message. If your name or the firm's name is familiar, your recipients will then go ahead and read the subject line.

If you are marketing to a list that doesn't know who you are, consider partnering with a publication or other partner whose name would be recognized by the target list.

Write truthful, accurate subject lines.
This may make it challenging to be catchy or provocative, but it lets the recipients know exactly what they will find when they open your message.

Include your contact information.
We strongly believe that your contact information (including your postal address and phone numbers) should be in the

signature file of all your outbound emails. It's like sending a letter on your letterhead instead of a blank piece of paper.

Make it easy to unsubscribe.
You must include a link or another easy way for recipients to opt out of receiving future email.

Don't let spam laws keep you from including email marketing as part of your marketing programs. As long as you know the laws, and employ proper strategies of effective email marketing, this valuable tool can help you turn good marketing programs into great ones.

What We Can Learn from Spam

You can learn a lot from spam. We all get those emails selling us everything from investment opportunities in Nigeria to enhancements of every kind. One thing is for sure: They wouldn't keep sending them if they didn't work.

As annoying as these emails are, their success indicates they have some elements of effectiveness that we marketers may be able to learn from. So how can these tactics make your opt-in email programs even stronger?

Here are a few ideas:

1. Your subject line is vital. If it isn't compelling, you'll get no further. Tell them why they can't afford to stop reading.

2. Brevity works. You don't need to pack every fact into each email. One key message per email should be your rule of thumb.

3. The proper frequency is critical. Sending just one piece usually doesn't work. But sending too often can backfire. A campaign that has a consistent, branded theme is always a great way to keep your message flowing.

4. Know your audience. Before you start, create a fictional profile of your typical buyer and try to speak directly to that person.

5. It's not about you, so cut straight to the benefits. No one cares about your history or how beautiful your offices are. They just want to know what you can do for them.

Naturally, we are not endorsing that you start sending spam. But there's no reason why you can't borrow some proven e-marketing techniques to shore up your email marketing program. Just remember to use your new knowledge for good, not evil!

How to Create a Successful Outbound Email Campaign

When you check your inbox, what do you typically see? If you're like most of us, you see way too many unwanted emails.

Outbound email campaigns can be powerful and cost-effective marketing tools. But how can your campaign break through the unwanted clutter and rise to the top? Here are some of the secrets we use to create successful outbound email campaigns.

First, mail either on Monday or Friday. We have found that mailing early in the week works best. Typically, Monday delivers the best results. Tuesday is second best, but in both cases an early morning delivery ensures an even better receptivity. According to a recent study, both reading of email and click-through rates are the highest on Monday and decline as the week goes on. However, the study also found that sometimes an upward trend exists on Fridays.

The explanation: On Monday, people are fresh and haven't gotten buried under a pile of work yet, so they're more willing to read and follow through with email offers. By Friday, people are upbeat, thinking about the weekend, so they get a bit more responsive. Our experience with successful email programs supports this study.

But, as you may guess, there's much more to conducting a successful email campaign. Here are a few more tips we strongly recommend:

1. Lead with a clear subject line. Your reader won't open the email if they don't know what the subject is. Don't try to be

too clever – just be clear.

2. Make sure you make your offer quickly. No matter what day of the week, people want you to get to the point quickly.

3. Repeat your offer. Don't just mention it once. We know people are skimming email, so repeat your offer in slightly different words at least twice in your email.

4. Include multiple opportunities for readers to click-through for more information. Have just one click-through landing page, but provide the link to it more than once.

5. Use bullet points, boxes and stand-alone sentences to guide your reader quickly through your info from most important to least important. If there is an expiration date, quantity limit or other critical fact, don't bury it at the end.

Outbound email is a powerful and cost-effective marketing tool. When used properly, it can add a significant boost to your marketing programs.

Email Marketing – Crafting Your Subject Line

There are many elements to creating effective online email marketing campaigns. Let's focus on the most important element – the subject line. In email marketing, the old saying "you never get a second chance to make a first impression" has never been more true.

A captivating and attention-grabbing subject line can make the difference between a hugely successful email campaign and one that falls flat on its face. So here are some tips to think about when crafting your email subject line...

- o Put yourself in your target's shoes. What's in it for them? Think of a strong, hard-to-refuse offer.

- o Keep it simple. The decision to either open or delete your email message is made by the recipient in less than three seconds.

- o Keep it short. Typically, you only have 30 to 40 characters to work with (including spaces), so make sure that your message is succinct.

- o Incorporate a specific benefit. Using a general statement such as "Grow holiday sales" typically won't work as well as a specific statement like "Free 30-day trial." Make sure that your statement is believable, avoiding statements along the lines of "Lose fat. No exercise," "Earn $10,000 per month," "Big money maker."

- o Craft your subject line so that the most critical words are first, to ensure they don't get cut off.

o Use capitalization judiciously. When you use all capital letters, there is no differentiation between your words, making them much harder to read. And, according to email etiquette, all caps means you're yelling!

o And finally, be sure to test. Often, what works with one target audience doesn't work as well for another. Using web analytics can tell you which emails are reaching your audience and turning into sales.

Although there are many other factors that can affect your results, the subject line is the easiest and most cost-effective variable to test first.

Creating Powerful E-messaging Programs (Part 1 of 2)

We are finding that the more successful marketing programs that we have created for our clients include an online e-messaging or e-newsletter component. Our very own *Marketing Smart*™ newsletter is a good example of the type of e-message we are describing to effectively deliver a specific marketing message.

This powerful marketing tactic allows you to deliver a specific marketing message to a specific audience. It may be one of the most powerful and cost-effective tools available to you. Therefore, if your marketing plan does not include this strategy then you may be missing out on a very low-cost opportunity to speak to your customers and prospects.

So what's the secret to creating a powerful e-messaging strategy? Before you sit down with your agency to develop your new plan, consider the following recommendations:

o   Content is king. If you do not provide something of value on a consistent basis, you may get them to sign up, but they'll never stay.

o   Be brief. Make it something they can scan and absorb in about 90 seconds.

o   Keep the horn tooting to a minimum. If it looks like one big ad for you and it sounds like one big ad for you, then it most likely is one big ad for you and... they won't keep reading.

o   Make sure the information is relevant and timely.

Provide your readers with information you know they want to know.

o   Send it out on a very regular basis and make sure that it always goes out, come rain or shine, on that same date.

o   And always deliver your message in a well-designed template to reinforce your branded look.

Without a doubt, when it comes to e-messaging, if you continue to deliver value and good information to your readers, they will find you, stay with you and ultimately turn to you when they need your product or service. By creating a loyal following of e-readers, you will not only keep your company name in front of your customers and prospects cost effectively, but you will position yourself as a trusted industry expert as well.

Creating Powerful E-messaging Programs (Part 2 of 2)

An online e-messaging program can be a very powerful and cost-effective marketing tool. Now let's outline the best way to develop a good email target list and attract more subscribers.

First of all, existing customers should be the first additions to your list. New prospects have to see the value in what you are providing to want to subscribe. And they need to know that you will not misuse their contact information. Also, be sure to get permission from each subscriber. So what are the key motivators for getting more prospects to sign up?

A recent survey best reflects the primary motivating factors for signing up for an e-messaging program.

- o Sweepstakes or chance to win a related product or service
- o Already a customer and/or have a favorably predisposed image
- o Email address required to access valued content
- o Referral/recommendation

This study also discovered why most e-messaging programs fail and why subscribers opt out of these programs.

- o Emails come too frequently
- o Lost interest in product/service/topic
- o Emails generally boring
- o Emails offered no significant value
- o Suspected company of sharing address

The best strategy to build your ongoing list is to be honest with your subscribers, provide them with valuable information and never compromise their trust in you. You should also invite your subscribers to share your information with others. Try offering some of your content to other related e-messages or e-newsletters with a byline and web link to your subscription page in exchange.

E-messaging programs are a very powerful and cost-effective component of our clients' marketing programs. Use them wisely and you too can reap the benefits of this powerful marketing strategy.

Key Words to Avoid in Your Next Email

Email marketing is a very powerful tool. It not only allows you to speak to your customers and prospects one-to-one, but it is very cost effective as well.

One of the major challenges now facing online marketing comes from spam filters and your ability to create email messages that make it through to your target. ISPs such as Yahoo, MSN, AOL and others block millions of email messages every day based on the content of the message. These spam filters look closely at the specific words you use in your subject lines as well as the body of the messages themselves.

In an effort to help you get more of your messages past these sophisticated filters and into the inboxes of your customers and prospects, the following is a list of commonly used words and phrases that most of these filters typically flag as spam.

Words to avoid:

- o   As seen on
- o   Buy direct
- o   Get paid
- o   Order now
- o   Please read
- o   Don't delete
- o   Time limited
- o   While supplies last
- o   Why pay more
- o   Special promotion
- o   Save up to
- o   All natural

- You've been selected
- Free
- Act now
- All new
- __% off
- Call now
- Subscribe now
- Earn money
- Discount
- Double your income
- You're a winner
- Information you requested
- Stop
- No cost
- No fees
- Opportunity
- Million dollars
- Compare
- Removes
- Collect
- Amazing
- Promise you
- Credit
- Loans
- Satisfaction guaranteed
- Search engine listings
- Join millions

If you try to avoid the words and phrases outlined above, you will find that your online delivery rates will increase.

Knowing Email Marketing Etiquette Can Create Big Results

There are no formal rules when it comes to email marketing etiquette. The one trend that we are seeing more is that good email marketing etiquette can make a big difference in how your customers respond to you and how they perceive your brand.

Email marketing etiquette can be critical to building a healthy, legitimate and reciprocal relationship with your customers and prospects. So how do you implement some of these tactics into your email programs? The following are some of the basic rules that we have found to be effective when it comes to email marketing etiquette:

Ask for permission – Permission is powerful. When a prospect or customer tells you that it is okay to send them something, then they will take your email more seriously than if you do not get their permission. Try to work into your general marketing programs a strategy that allows you to get permission (or opt in) from your customers or prospects.

Confidentiality – Be sure that you clearly post your confidentiality policy. Most email subscribers are concerned about their email address getting into the wrong hands or being bombarded with unwanted emails. Let them know what they can expect from you and what you will be doing with their email address. The greatest results come when you are honest with them. We recommend that you post your confidentiality policy, or a link to it, near your opt-in request box.

Give them a way out – Just as you should make it easy for them to opt in, make it easy for them to opt out. Just having a clear and functional unsubscribe option puts your reader at ease, and lets them know that you are professional and value their time.

Provide a confirmation – Each time someone opts in or out, be sure that you send a prompt confirmation. This should be a simple, automated response, ideally within a few minutes of their request. We always suggest that your message include a brief note, such as "Thanks for subscribing to Gumas' *Marketing Smart*™. We look forward to providing you with valuable marketing knowledge each month."

Monitor activity closely – Be sure that you or your advertising agency manages your database closely and responds to all inquiries or complaints promptly. We too often see companies not utilizing email for its real benefit – the ability to speak one-to-one to your prospects and customers.

And, as with all proper etiquette, please don't forget to say please and thank you! Thank you.

Word-of-Mouth Marketing 101

As consumers, we have always relied on referrals – or warnings – from family and friends for everything from the best hotels and restaurants to accounting firms and ad agencies. But as conventional media becomes more fragmented, more and more marketers are trying to capture the power of a good referral.

With the fragmentation of conventional media, marketers should be looking for ways to enhance their referrals on a larger scale. This strategy is called word-of-mouth marketing.

A recent study of over 26,000 people found that 78% trusted "recommendations from other consumers," which, in turn, significantly increased the likelihood that the recommendation resulted in a purchase. These numbers are way too powerful for any marketer to ignore.

As interactive marketing gains more and more credibility, we are finding that there is an increasing interest among our clients concerning ways to incorporate referrals or word-of-mouth marketing into their marketing campaigns. So what is word-of-mouth marketing? Since the interactive portion of this is such an emerging field, not everyone agrees on the answer, but the following are some examples:

- o **Buzz marketing** – Using high-profile news or entertainment to get people to talk about your brand.

- o **Viral marketing** – Creating entertaining or informative messages that are designed to be passed along at an exponential rate, often online or by email.

o **Community marketing** – Forming or supporting niche communities that are likely to share interests about your brand (such as user groups, fan clubs and discussion forums); providing tools, content and information to those communities.

o **Grassroots marketing** – Organizing and motivating volunteers to engage in personal or local outreach.

o **Evangelist marketing** – Cultivating evangelists, advocates or volunteers who are encouraged to take a leadership role in actively spreading the word on your behalf.

o **Product seeding** – Placing the right product into the right hands at the right time, providing information or samples to influential individuals who, in turn, share their experiences with the product.

o **Influencer marketing** – Identifying key communities and opinion leaders who are likely to talk about products and have the ability to influence the opinions of others, including the press or industry analysts.

o **Cause marketing** – Supporting local social causes to earn the respect and support of people who feel strongly about the cause.

o **Conversational creation** – Interesting or fun advertising, catchphrases, entertainment, emails or promotions designed to start word-of-mouth activity.

o **Brand blogging** – Creating blogs and participating in

the blogosphere in the spirit of open, transparent communications; sharing information of value that the blog community may talk about.

o **Referral programs –** Creating tools that enable satisfied customers to refer their friends. Email and other interactive methodologies are ways to offer innovative referral programs.

Now that you know some different types of word-of-mouth marketing, what can you do to start implementing it at your company?

NOTES:

The ABCs of Viral Marketing
(Part 1 of 3)

Even though everyone talks about viral marketing like it's a new type of online marketing tactic, it has actually been around for a very long time. Viral marketing can be anything from handing out free samples at the grocery store to dropping wallets throughout a targeted geographic area and loading each one with a card directing the finder to a website to see if they have won the million dollar reward.

Today, when most people hear the term "viral" they assume it has something to do with online media or social networking. Oftentimes, it does.

Viral marketing is basically any marketing effort that you "release" into the marketplace and let chart its own course. The key element of viral marketing is that you relinquish control to the consumers and let them take the campaign where they see fit.

It's possible and often advantageous to use an element of viral marketing in almost every campaign you do. In fact, we've been including viral elements into our clients' campaigns for years. The only difference is, the Internet has now made our options much broader and more cost efficient.

A common misconception is that viral marketing is only for the young. While 15 to 25 year olds are clearly frequent Internet users, so are many other target groups, such as business executives, general consumers and even many seniors.

The key to viral marketing is matching your messaging to the needs of your target audience.

NOTES:

The ABCs of Viral Marketing
(Part 2 of 3)

In Part 1, we described the basics of a viral marketing campaign. We described it as a marketing program that you release into the marketplace and let the marketplace chart its course. In this second part, we will explore the mindset needed to make a viral campaign successful.

Viral marketing is not typical. In fact, many aspects of it go against the basics of most marketing strategies. So in order to have a successful viral campaign, you need to do the following:

Have the right mindset – It sounds great in theory, but giving up control over a major portion of your marketing campaign is not always easy. How will you respond the first time a customer starts to criticize your product in their blog or talks about your slow service? Or you end up on the news because someone thinks you're subversive? Since you can't control where it goes, it takes a thick skin to utilize viral marketing.

You need the courage of a lion – Viral marketing quickly takes on a life of its own. It's like releasing a butterfly. Once you open the cage, it's not likely you are going to get the butterfly to return. The ride is always interesting, but seldom smooth. And there's nothing worse than being in the middle of a viral campaign, having your CEO get cold feet and then try to reel it all back in. That will not only destroy the campaign but most likely cause a public relations nightmare.

You have no control of time – Sometimes they launch like a rocket, but more often they take days or months to build up momentum. So if you are in a hurry or have a time-sensitive message, this might not be the right tool to use.

You can't be predictable – The one thing that will certainly sink your viral campaign is predictability. You can't do things like everyone else. You have to come up with ideas that are unique to your audience.

You need the spirit of a gambler – Viral marketing comes with no guarantees. Your idea can either fall flat on its face or launch your company to the next level. There's no "pay-for-play," but just a good old-fashioned "spin-of-the-wheel."

The ABCs of Viral Marketing
(Part 3 of 3)

In the prior two parts, we outlined the elements of viral marketing and what you need to make it successful. Now we will outline how to measure your campaign's effectiveness.

Measuring a successful viral marketing campaign can be difficult because viral marketing is a whole other breed of animal. When we do our analysis of our viral campaigns, we break them into three distinct phases, each phase having its own form of measurement. The following is our process:

Phase 1 – Start-up: This phase is all about measuring buzz and awareness. Is anyone talking about your campaign? Has the local media covered it? Is traffic on your website, blog or landing page beginning to grow? Are you seeing the right prospects coming to your site?

Phase 2 – Growth: This is where your viral campaign has hit critical mass and is growing. In this phase, you need to measure your campaign's frequency, such as how many free demos were downloaded, how many people came to your location, the number of unique page views to your blog, etc. You want to know how many people have responded and how often they are coming back.

Phase 3 – Wind-up: This final phase is all about how long your viral campaign can last. Is your community as vibrant as it was six months ago? Some viral campaigns are designed to burn out quickly, while others can sustain themselves for many years. At this phase you need to measure the long-term impact of your relationships. How often do they buy? Who have they referred?

Are they an influencer that drives direct sales?

Typically, the results in a viral campaign are slower and more difficult to measure than a traditional campaign, but the relationship formed with the customer is deeper.

Why? Because viral marketing is about creating a relationship between your company and its customers. Relationships take time to mature and bear fruit. But in the long run, having a loyal customer who feels a connection to you sure beats the price shopper or the "what have you done for me lately" type of customer.

The Keys to Effective Paid Search Advertising

We all do it. In fact, some of us do it many times a day. We go onto Google, Yahoo or one of the many other search engines available, looking for products and services that we need.

What comes back to us is a list of companies that can fulfill our need. Now look at these results from the perspective of your business goals... wouldn't it be great to have a spot on the first page of people's search engine results? Since market research shows that 90% of searches do not go beyond the first page of results, being on page one is invaluable.

Well you can. It's called paid search. For mere pennies, you can get in front of prospects searching the web for your product or service by buying keywords. When those keywords are typed in, you will appear as a sponsored link or in a higher position in the regular listings.

Sounds great – but if you don't know how to do it right, it can become an expensive experiment. So here are some of the strategies we use when conducting cost-effective search campaigns for our clients:

Be specific. If you choose a very generic word or phrase like "building" or "golf clubs," you could be paying a lot of extra money for clicks that are completely irrelevant to your business. Instead of "building," consider "new luxury condos in San Francisco." Instead of "golf clubs," try "performance fairway woods." The more specific, the better.

Listen. When you talk to your customers, pay attention to how they talk. Do they ask for luxury condos or high-rise living? Do they need a fairway wood or a fairway metal? Use their language, because they search the same way they talk.

Try some good old-fashioned espionage. Start by researching your own site to see what words and phrases your prospects are currently using to find you. Also do this same exercise on your competitors' sites. This information will be very helpful and eye opening.

Keep modifying. The best part of search marketing is that it is 100% trackable. This means that you can continually test which words or phrases are generating the best results and modify them accordingly. So experiment with different combinations or synonyms of critical words that generate the best results.

There are very few true marketing techniques that are trackable. Search listings can be a very powerful and cost-effective tool to drive prospects that are looking to buy right to your door.

NOTES:

SECTION 7—TRADESHOWS, PR & OTHER STUFF

Once your marketing machine is up and running, keep the momentum going and strengthen your brand by raising your profile and making yourself a credible expert at the forefront of your industry.

Tradeshows – Are They Worth the Investment? (Part 1 of 2)

Tradeshows can be expensive. But are they worth the investment of your company's money and your staff's time? Depending on your specific business and marketing tactics, we find that tradeshows can be a very powerful marketing tool, if executed correctly.

Tradeshows are a great way to renew relationships with existing or old customers, make an immediate impression on many potential customers in a relatively short period of time and establish direct contact with people important to your business. Tradeshows bring an entire industry together to showcase the latest and greatest, as well as the tried and true. With speaking programs, exhibit booths, parties and more, they offer endless ways to connect with the movers and shakers in that particular industry.

For your new-business efforts, gaining new contacts can be another important benefit. Tradeshows bring together large numbers of potential customers and allow you to expose your products and services to them. In effect, a tradeshow allows you to speak to many months' worth of customers in just a few days.

In so many ways, tradeshows can be a powerful component of your company's marketing activities. Properly executed, they will produce huge returns in exposure, branding, education and sales. The return on investment that you can expect from your tradeshow activities is typically correlated to the amount of effort and strategic planning you put into them. So what should you do to maximize your tradeshow opportunities? Here are some strategies that have helped many of our clients generate huge returns:

1. Develop a pre-show plan.
This may be the most critical aspect of successful tradeshow marketing. Before you attend a tradeshow, develop an outline of what you want to accomplish. Why are you attending and what type of results do you hope to achieve? Sales? Product education? Product demonstration? Company exposure?

2. Target prospects early on.
If your objective is to meet with potential customers, consider creating a list in advance of these target prospects. Before the show begins, send a personalized letter to each asking for an appointment. Another approach is to simply use the letter to tell them what you can do for them and to give them an incentive to come by your booth to meet you. The objective is to get on your prospects' radar screens before the tradeshow begins, so that you can productively spend your time at the show speaking to those individuals who can generate the most business for you.

3. Practice before you go.
Before you go to the tradeshow, take your show staff aside and practice. Practice where everyone will be and what they will say to a potential prospect. What's their opening line? What materials will they hand out? What will they do if the prospect is interested? How will they gather prospect information for follow-up? Remember, you have just a couple of days to get a year's worth of work done. Things will be happening fast and furiously, so make sure that everyone understands their roles ahead of time.

Keep in mind that in addition to new-business outreach, tradeshows can offer much in professional development and provide an understanding of your industry that you just can't get elsewhere. Oftentimes, editors of key industry publications are there making new connections for advertising and editorial space. A tradeshow can be the spark that ignites your efforts for the next year, so it's best to use your time wisely. In Part 2, we'll look at more ways to maximize your tradeshow experience – before, during and after.

NOTES:

Tradeshows – Are They Worth the Investment? (Part 2 of 2)

Tradeshows are a great way to gain a comprehensive understanding of your industry in a weekend. But do they make sense in terms of the staff and budget needed for a larger presence?

In Part 1, we looked at preparation for tradeshows, a crucial aspect of making the most of your commitment. Here are more ways to maximize your experience:

1. Get your staff on the same page.
Before the show begins, train each person who will staff your booth. Be sure that everyone knows your objectives, policies and sales procedures. And make sure that they all understand your product line and how best to sell those products in a fast-paced tradeshow environment.

Remember, selling at a tradeshow is very different than selling in a retail or direct environment. At a tradeshow, you typically have just a few seconds to attract the interest of a busy attendee. Time is limited. Don't be so anxious to close a sale at the show that you cause the prospect to sense your anxiety and back away. It's okay to set up the sale for the future as long as you conclude the tradeshow contact with an appropriate action plan in place. And let the prospect be an active participant in the development of that action plan.

2. Draw potential customers into your booth.
You typically have about three seconds to grab prospects' attention as they walk past your tradeshow booth. So how do you get them to stop and listen?

Be strategically creative. We don't recommend giving away promotional items unless the prospects do something to earn them. Invite prospects into your booth for a presentation or product demo. As an incentive, offer them something as a reward. T-shirts with your logo and/or sales message are popular, and offer good promotional exposure as well. Then collect each prospect's name, address, email address and other vital information for subsequent follow-up.

3. Organize your notes.

You can't possibly remember every conversation with every prospective customer, so take notes on the prospect's business card or whatever other contact form you've developed. Rank each contact as to the likelihood and readiness to buy. A letter or number code works well for this purpose. For example, A – "very hot prospect," B = "a good prospect," etc. Include any additional follow-up information. Make sure that everyone who staffs your booth uses the same code.

4. Post-show follow-up.

Once the tradeshow is over, the real marketing activity should begin. Have a plan in place to follow up with all contacts immediately. Organize your notes, which should indicate each person's apparent level of interest at the time you spoke with them, from hot to cool. Concentrate your follow-up efforts on the hottest prospects first, but be sure to follow up with every prospect, no matter how routine it may seem. Branding impressions are formed incrementally over time, through every contact a prospect or customer has with your company. Tradeshow contacts are no exception. Therefore, failure to follow up as promised can create a devastating impression.

Some statistics on the average tradeshow attendee:
- o   95% asked for literature to be sent
- o   95% saw and spoke to a current supplier
- o   94% compared similar products
- o   77% found at least one supplier
- o   76% asked for a price/quote
- o   51% requested a sales rep call
- o   26% signed a purchase order

Tradeshows are a great way to build awareness and generate sales. But, as with all marketing activity, the better you plan and integrate your tradeshow strategy into your overall marketing plan, the better results you can expect.

Consider your tradeshow efforts as a complete marketing package with before, during and after strategies, and watch your return on investment dramatically increase.

NOTES:

Are You Satisfied with Your Tradeshow ROI?

Tradeshows are a great way to penetrate a market, build a company and generate new sales leads. Yet most of the companies we speak with feel that they do not get the results they would like to see from their tradeshow investment.

Just going to a tradeshow is generally better than not going at all. But, if you do them right, tradeshows should contribute significantly to your overall marketing success.

So what does "do them right" mean? While time and space will not permit a full exploration of the pre-, during- and post-show strategies we recommend to our clients, we have compiled a short list of the most important tactics to consider in helping you enhance your tradeshow success.

What's your point?
As prospects walk through a tradeshow floor, remember they are distracted. They're not thinking of you; they are thinking of themselves. So think of your booth as a billboard. Have only one message that speaks directly to your prospects' needs and gets them to stop in their tracks. Make sure this message has a theme that ties directly to your brand.

Get them into your booth.
If your prospects don't stop and walk into your booth, you'll never be able to speak with them. So have a plan in place to make this happen. Offer them something if they sit through a short presentation. Do something in your booth that will capture their attention. This is not the time or the place to be shy. Again, just make sure that what you do ties into your theme and/or brand.

Do it right.

First impressions are powerful. They directly reflect the perceived image of your company's brand. Tradeshows can deliver some of the most qualified prospects you could ever wish for. So don't leave that first impression to chance. Make sure that your overall image, message and display reflects the quality of your organization's brand. You shouldn't be cutting corners.

Capture names and follow up after the show.

Sounds like a simple and obvious thing to do. But we can't tell you how many times we have seen companies that have no data-capturing system or follow-up plan in place. Develop a comprehensive plan before you go to the show. Make sure everyone in your booth knows what the plan is. And then execute that plan immediately upon your return from the show.

Maximizing Tradeshow Returns

Many companies spend huge amounts of money each year on tradeshows. But are they really getting the best return on their investment?

Tradeshows can be a very effective strategy in reaching your target audience. However, as with any marketing vehicle, you are fighting with numerous competitors for the attention of the same audience. Here are some suggestions to help maximize your efforts.

1. Don't think of a tradeshow as a stand-alone marketing vehicle. Integrate it with your other marketing efforts such as ads, websites and direct mail. Tell your customers and prospects in advance that you'll be at the show, and give them a reason to visit your booth.

2. If you have business partners at the same show, try cross-promoting each other. Do joint giveaways and promotions that require visits to both booths, or simply create a promotional piece that highlights your combined services.

3. Your exhibit signage should clearly define whom you are, what you do and whom you want to talk to. And it should get this information across in five seconds or less. This will eliminate those who are not your target audience, so that you can speak to the right people. Don't try to be everything to everyone. Niche yourself.

4. Try giving your target audience an incentive for sitting through a presentation. What's it worth to your company to have the undivided attention of potential prospects for ten

minutes? Be creative.

5. Be sure to have a plan in place to immediately follow up on all leads generated from the show.

With a little effort and creativity, tradeshows can become a powerful marketing tool.

Want to Get Some Good PR?

Are you looking for ways to get more awareness and exposure for your company or products without having to spend a lot of money? (Well, who isn't?) Consider this public relations tactic.

Try packaging your message as a learning experience for a targeted publication's readers. For example, a software company might offer an article on how and when to implement software upgrades to maximize productivity and minimize downtime. A bank might offer an article on teaching kids the best ways to handle money. Or a builder might offer decorating tips to help make your home more energy efficient. You get the picture. You just need to be creative.

Editors are hungry for good articles that teach their readers how to solve a problem. These "how-to" articles are one of the best ways to promote yourself to the audience you are targeting. In fact, you can even customize your article for different audiences and different publications.

When your name and company is recognized as the author of an article, it gives you immediate credibility as an expert. Best of all, when you reprint these articles, they can provide you with powerful marketing materials that will be worth their weight in gold.

NOTES:

The Five Basics of Effective Newsletters

Newsletters are a proven marketing tool. Done properly, they can be a very powerful weapon in your marketing arsenal. Unfortunately, most newsletter efforts fall short and typically end up in their reader's circular file. Why? Because they don't follow the basics of effective newsletters.

We have developed some basic rules when we create newsletters for our clients. The following are what we believe to be the five most important rules of effective newsletter marketing:

1. Have a plan and a vision.
Your newsletter needs to have a plan and a vision. Without either, it is destined to become a hodge-podge of articles that have no continuity or purpose. Make sure you identify your newsletter's key audiences and what you want them to do or know. It's very difficult to build reader loyalty without an understanding of what your readers want.

2. Go light on the ego.
Your newsletter is a sales tool. But be careful that you don't toot your horn to the point of arrogance. It's good to celebrate your product's/service's excellence, but try doing it with case studies or client testimonials rather than in the first person. It's simply more credible this way.

3. Provide value to your reader.
Your reader only cares about one thing: "What's in it for me?" Your newsletter is fighting for your audience's most precious asset – their time. So be sure you make it worth their time to read. Give them new information or valuable insights so they will look forward to receiving your next issue.

4. Be consistent.

Hitting deadlines is difficult, but be sure you always meet those deadlines. If you promise a monthly or quarterly newsletter, then be sure that you deliver a monthly or quarterly newsletter on time, every time. What do you think it says about your company if you can't keep your promise to deliver your newsletter on time?

5. Make it interactive.

Encourage your readers to talk back or ask questions. If you send an electronic newsletter, provide them an easy link to ask questions or provide feedback. If you opt for a traditional printed newsletter, provide an email address, a bounce back card or a special URL that solicits feedback. And always try to make it a conversation rather than a monologue.

Newsletters are a lot of work. But all this work can translate into powerful brand-building results and sales results. Make sure that you incorporate these five basic rules into your newsletter and you'll have loyal readers for a long time to come.

The Seven Words or Phrases You Should Never Use in a Press Release

A strong public relations strategy should always work hand-in-hand with your overall marketing and advertising strategy. The key to successful public relations is identifying the right "story hook" for the right media outlet and then presenting that story correctly to the press.

Where we see most companies' public relations efforts stray off course is not only in their overall strategy but also within the wording of their press releases.

As a whole, the press is an intelligent, above-average group. So when you, or your marketing firm, write your press releases, be sure that you stick to the facts with as little embellishment as possible.

With that said, here are the seven words or phrases that you should never include in a press release:

1. Industry-leading
2. Unique
3. Cutting-edge
4. Breakthrough
5. Revolutionary
6. World-class
7. The Best

Remember that you are writing news, not a print ad. The press is very factual. They report on the who, what, where, when and why. We have found that they will respond better to your releases when you provide them with just that.

NOTES:

How to Create a Winning Presentation

It doesn't matter what department you're in. It doesn't even matter what your job title is. The fact is we all have to make presentations at some point in our careers. We make them to boards of directors. We make them to prospective clients. We make them to internal staff. Some presentations are casual and some are formal. With each presentation, there is typically a lot riding on your ability to convince the audience you are addressing.

So what can you do to improve your presentation skills? The following suggestions may help:

1. Do a little research.
Know your audience. Who will be attending? What are their issues and concerns? The more you can tailor your presentation to your audience's specific needs, the more impact you will make.

2. Engage your audience.
Don't let your audience get bored. Keep them engaged. If possible, make your presentation interactive. For example, involve those on the receiving end of your talk by asking questions and having them shout out answers.

3. Make it interesting.
Have you ever sat through a presentation of facts and figures? It's not too long before you start dreaming of that "happy place." Don't let this happen to you. Make your presentation interesting by illustrating your points through stories, famous quotes or metaphors and analogies that your audience can relate to.

4. Make the information relevant.

Ask yourself, "Why should my audience care?" Good presentations should be relevant to the audience, not the speaker. To hook observers into your message, include nuggets of information that they won't have heard before or be able to find elsewhere. You'll leave a lasting impression by providing necessary information they can chew on afterwards.

5. Keep your visuals simple.

Visuals can "break up" a presentation in a good way – saying with simple images what you can't say with many words. They also add a professional polish that can move your message one level beyond the norm. Whether you are using PowerPoint or good old-fashioned flip charts, make sure that your visuals are simple to understand. Use them to emphasize key points and not to outline your entire presentation.

6. Show some passion.

The more dynamic you are, the more powerful your presentation will be. Demonstrate the passion you have through your facial expressions, the tone of your voice and your hand gestures. And always make eye contact with your audience. If you are finding it hard to put passion into dry material, ask yourself why it matters, who benefits or why you are singling it out among many things you could talk about. Even the driest material can be put forth passionately when you care about it.

7. Dress the part.

The way you dress should establish credibility and should never become a focal point for your audience. If your audience focuses on something you are wearing or the overall way you are dressed, they will get distracted from your message. Remember that you never get a second chance to make a first impression.

When in doubt, buy a new suit or ask someone's advice on what to wear.

8. Be prepared.
Yes, this is an obvious one. But the simple fact remains that the better prepared you are, the better your presentation will be. It never hurts to practice a few times before doing it for real.

9. Be your own best judge.
Use yourself as a test case – if you're not being entertained and enjoying giving your presentation, there's virtually no way your audience is enjoying receiving it. Conversely, when you're feeling good about your content and overall presentation, your audience is too. Lastly, most people have a fear of public speaking. There's only one way to get over it – by doing it again and again. Each time, it will get easier, and you'll find yourself learning more about this critical aspect of professional life.

NOTES:

Stand Up Tall On That Soap Box

Offering your expertise as a guest speaker is an excellent way to introduce yourself, your company and your products or services to potential customers. You have immediate credibility and a captive, pre-qualified audience. So how do you make the most of this type of opportunity?

First, it's not a presentation. So try to go easy on the self-promotion. You've been asked to speak because you are an expert. Talk about ideas, insights and the marketplace. Give them information they can use. That doesn't mean you can't talk about yourself, but do it in the context of your case studies or examples.

Don't forget about the audience. Are they middle-level managers? C-level executives? Business owners? Also, be sure to find out where you are in the program. Is it an all-day meeting and you're the 3:00 speaker? Or are you the first one of the day? These tidbits of information should help you craft a presentation with the right information, tone and energy level.

Once you know whom you're talking to and what you're going to say, try to avoid gimmicks or A/V tricks. Sure, PowerPoint works great to highlight some facts or enhance some visuals. But just standing there reading the slides to them is not going to make anyone ohh and ahh about your expertise. And besides, if they fall asleep, they'll never hear what you have to say.

Think about the presentations that you really enjoyed and talked about afterward – they were engaging, insightful, and they connected on a personal level. You didn't feel preached to or a hard-sell push. If you think in those terms – that you are there to share yourself, the business will come naturally, as will more speaking invitations!

Do You Know How to Speak to the Press?

There's no advertising exposure more credible than having a PR story featuring your company or product in a magazine, local newspaper or on television or radio.

Many times, our clients will ask us to help train them to become better at the interview process. They ask us to teach them that special interview "style" or how to best "perform" for reporters. Here's the advice we've been giving our clients for the last 25 years…

Many reporters will make immediate judgments about you based on your body language, tone of voice and other small nuances that determine your honesty, integrity and depth of knowledge. So our advice is always the same: be yourself, act naturally and come to the interview with a clear message that will be interesting to the reporters' audience. The more you try to be someone you are not, the less credible you appear in the eyes of professional reporters.

With that caveat, here are five tips to keep in mind the next time the press is interviewing you:

1. Be prepared. Practice your message until it sounds natural and unrehearsed. The best way to do well in an interview is to know what you want to say beforehand. Have your main message points written down and in front of you so you can be sure to cover these main topics.
2. Speak at a slower pace. Most of us tend to speak faster when we're nervous, so be sure to slow down.
3. Keep your answers informal, conversational and try not to speak in techno-babble. You'll come across as more

believable.

4. If you get off-track from what you intended to say or get hit with a difficult question, answer it as briefly as possible and politely move the discussion back to your key points. For example: "Yes, we've had layoffs, but the good news for our company and our community is (insert your key message here)."

5. Relax and be yourself.

PR coverage is a great tool for any company. If you don't have an ongoing PR plan already, be sure to develop one, and learn to speak to the press. Then just watch your company grow.

Does Your Company Dress for Success?

When it comes to the successful marketing of an organization, sometimes it's the little details that can make a huge difference. For example, the next time you walk into a new home showroom, retail store or any other place of business, take a look around at what the employees are wearing. Think about the feeling you get from those businesses where no one seems to care about what they're wearing. Now, compare that to the feeling you get when you walk into a business where each employee is wearing a company uniform or identifiable clothing.

A recent study provided some very interesting insight into what consumers expect and their level of comfort when it comes to consistent dress and uniforms. This study found that customers spent an average of 27% more when they purchased from uniformed employees versus companies whose representatives were not wearing uniforms. In addition, the branding and perception value toward the uniformed businesses was also significantly larger than that of the non-uniformed businesses.

This particular study involved both mid- and large-sized organizations that had various retail-type operations. About 50% of the companies agreed to use uniformed sales staff, while the other 50% did not.

Another similar uniform study was recently conducted by a large national bank. Everyone in the organization, from tellers to the bank management, started wearing company logo shirts. Through this simple change in dress policy, they found that customers' positive attitudes towards the bank, and bank sales, increased during the test period. They also found that customer loyalty and brand recognition increased.

Large retailers like Target, Kmart and Sears have also taken notice of these studies and have mandated logoed golf shirts as a uniform for all their employees.

How do you define uniform?
Many people have a preconceived image of what a uniform means. Company uniforms do not have to look like employees are ready to pump gas. They can simply be shirts of the same color embroidered with your corporate logo. However you define "uniform," a corporate uniform is simply a way to make your company look professional, brand-consistent and identifiable to the customer.

Obviously, uniforms are not practical for every company. But take a moment to look deeper into what these findings are saying. Customers see this as a real effort to make them feel appreciated. Also, this is a great way to reinforce your brand at point of sale.

The obvious items that come to mind include logoed shirts, hats, jackets and other similar apparel. But what about logoed coffee mugs on everyone's desk in the sales office and in the conference room for clients to use? Or a logoed carpet when clients arrive in your sales office or lobby? How about logoed note pads for your clients to use and take with them?

Try to brainstorm on how your company could reinforce your brand image by having your employees and/or sales teams wear or use something that further builds your brand.

Be creative. Uniforms don't always have to be worn, but they can be a part of your clients' daily exposure to your organization and its brand. Branding is a process that includes multiple touch-points with your prospects and clients. And, sometimes, it's the attention to the smaller branding details that is just as important as your mainstream advertising and branding efforts.

NOTES:

Your Product Oughta Be in Pictures

Remember that great scene from the movie *E.T.*, when E.T. was eating Reese's Pieces? Or how about that great episode of *Seinfeld* when Kramer couldn't get enough of those great-tasting Junior Mints? What do you think happened to sales for both of these products shortly after their on-screen debuts? You probably guessed it… sales shot through the roof.

These perfectly placed product opportunities did not happen by accident. They were part of a well-developed, strategic marketing plan that included Product Placement as a supporting element.

By definition, Product Placement is the process of securing media exposure for your products or services in major movies and television productions. The value is that your product or service is embedded within the program or film and becomes associated with the story. In addition to the obvious immediate exposure, your product or service's exposure also travels with the film or TV show throughout its life in the ever-expanding global distribution channels, such as DVD releases or television re-runs.

When we get our clients' products placed on the big screen, we always like to create a promotion around the exposure for added impact. Press releases, client/staff viewing parties, website stories and other similar promotional support goes a long way to add to your Product Placement exposure and ensure it becomes a huge marketing hit for you.

So how do you get your name in the movies? There are many companies in this industry that can make this happen for you.

We caution that you be careful about which product placement firm you deal with, since some companies are more reputable than others. Also, we strongly suggest that Product Placement be a part of your overall marketing program and not just a one-off event in order to get the greatest return on your investment.

NOTES:

About the Author

John Gumas is the president of Gumas Advertising, an award-winning branding, advertising and interactive marketing agency he founded in 1984. A veteran of the advertising and marketing industry, John has built Gumas Advertising into a successful firm that works with a host of local, national and international clients.

John is a highly sought-after speaker and has given countless presentations on Challenger Brand marketing to his peers in the profession, companies, conferences, college students and, on occasion, his barber!

John currently sits on many boards, including the San Francisco Giants Community Fund, The San Francisco Chamber of Commerce, The San Francisco State University Foundation, The Greater San Francisco Advertising Club and The Elios Society. In addition, John is an adjunct professor of advertising and marketing, a regular columnist for numerous publications, an author and a frequent speaker.